Live UNTIL YOU DIE

LEAVING A LEGACY OF
COURAGE AND FAITH

Live UNTIL YOU DIE

LEAVING A LEGACY OF
COURAGE AND FAITH

RANDY L. BOTT

CFI
An imprint of Cedar Fort, Inc.
Springville, Utah

ISBN 13: 978-1-4621-3935-4

Published by CFI, an imprint of Cedar Fort, Inc.
2373 W. 700 S., Springville, UT 84663
Distributed by Cedar Fort, Inc., www.cedarfort.com

Library of Congress Control Number: 2021932850

Cover design by Courtney Proby

Printed in the United States of America

10 9 8 7 6 5 4 3 2 1

Printed on acid-free paper

Contents

Chapter 1

IF IT IS TO BE, WHY NOT START WITH ME?

In a world shrouded with death, destruction, uncertainty, and illness, it is easy to develop an attitude of helplessness and hopelessness. This book will not fall into those self-defeating mindsets. From the very onset of this book, you should know I am simultaneously an optimist and a pragmatist. Having worked with the terminally ill for a number of years and also being a professional educator for four decades, I may have had experiences that have forced me to look more closely at the process of dying than most people. I do not claim to have all the answers. Indeed, I do not even know all of the questions. However, if we wait until one comes who knows everything there is to know, he or she may well arrive after all of us have exited from this life.

You will notably detect a "next world" orientation to my writing. Having been a lay minister for most of my adult life has convinced me that life consists of a much greater spectrum than the narrow confines between birth and death. Although my orientation is religious, this book is not intended to be a theological treatise. Only Chapter 16: "On the Other Side of Death's Door" will deal directly with what the Holy Bible teaches about life after death.

From the very beginning of recorded history, God gave the command to Adam and Eve to "be fruitful, and multiply, and replenish the earth, and **subdue it**: and **have dominion over** the fish of the sea, and over the fowl of the air, and over every living thing that moveth upon the earth (Genesis 1:28, emphasis added).

Would a fair and loving God give a commandment that we are unable to keep? Webster defines "subdue" as "to conquer and bring into subjection; to bring under control especially by an exertion of the will." The dictionary definition of "dominion" is "domain; supreme authority; absolute ownership." Its synonym is "power." As we begin to explore the options available to us as we advance in age and as our physical and mental faculties begin to diminish, we may be consoled to realize that we (not the environment) are still very much in control. Perhaps aging is one of the supreme blessings of life. While we were young and foolish, we may have taken for granted our ability to command and have our bodies respond. Our minds were more like sponges, absorbing information at an admirable rate. Many will remember the days when we were too smart to be taught because we knew everything there was to know. Heaven only knows how much more than our parents we had learned before we even exited the teenage years.

One of the blessings of growing older is the ability to realize and prize the physical and mental resources we really have. No longer do we run to the top of a mountain to enjoy the sunrise. We may still get there, but it may be more to enjoy the sunset or the heat of the day. As children run by us on the trails, they may arrive at the top of the mountain long before us, but almost all of them have missed the beauty of the wildflowers, the bugs and insects, the animals and birds, the breathless beauty of the waterfall, or the puffy, lazy white clouds that float effortlessly in the azure sky above us. It may even be that we never make it to the top of the mountain, but the rewards found at the lower levels far offset the panoramic view we had to forfeit because our legs and lungs would not take us to the summit. In fact, the times we are required to pause to catch our breath may be the most rewarding episodes of the entire journey.

Perhaps as children we may not have appreciated the muscles and flexibility we enjoyed. Now a very little unusual exertion results in our muscles and joints telling us loudly whether we are in condition to do the desired task. Sometimes it isn't until later that evening or even the next morning that we gain a real appreciation for the strength and flexibility of youth as our joints set up and our muscles cramp and rebel.

As pain becomes a more constant companion, it is tempting to take the easy road and not exert ourselves. That hardly sounds like a positive response to the initial command to "subdue" and take "dominion" over our world. As our population ages, more attention is being focused on the problems associated with old age. Doctors have concluded, documentaries have been produced, and living testimonials not a few are available to testify that it is never too late to get in better shape than we are in at the present.

Although there is almost always an invitation to "see your doctor before beginning any exercise program," the inference is that after consulting your doctor, you should be able to participate to the level of your abilities in some program of getting in better shape. It would not be wise to try to regain your youthful physical condition too quickly. Hopefully, the aging process has helped us learn to use more adult wisdom in metering our self-improvement program. There may indeed come a time when you will no longer be able to participate in strenuous outdoor activities. That time may be years after you originally thought. Give it a try and see if by increasing the amount you do by small incremental steps; you can't see self-rewarding progress almost immediately.

If we begin by telling ourselves it is impossible, chances are very high that we will become a self-fulfilling prophecy. Not that we can't accomplish our goal but that if we don't have faith and confidence in ourselves, we probably won't expend the energy and take the chance necessary to ensure success. So, the first thing to do is eliminate all the negative self-talk. Replace it with positive, reinforcing comments.

Since it is always more fun to do things with someone, find someone in about the same physical shape you are in and start together. If you have a spouse, chances are he or she is the one who will become your exercise partner. Start slow and work up. This old business of "no pain, no gain" may be fine if you are training for a marathon or a body-building contest, but for those of us who would just like a little more energy at the end of the day, that motto is pure garbage. You don't need to be sore and stiff after a workout session.

If you are in doubt as to how to start, there are community service organizations who would be more than willing to get you started. Nose around the senior citizen center, a church, the city and/or county offices, or other places the seniors might congregate. Be willing to ask questions, and don't be satisfied with non-committal answers.

Assuming you have either determined to improve your physical condition or are in relatively good shape, be willing to branch out into the other areas of life. Although a few suffer from mind-destroying or limiting diseases, most of us lose our ability to think and reason because we fail to use our minds on a regular basis. Anything from chess to "Wheel of Fortune" affords opportunities to stretch your mind. Books are a dime a dozen at a used bookstore. Although it is true that most books are not worth the paper they are written on, many great, mind-expanding books have been written and yet collect dust at the local libraries and bookstores. Book clubs organized by seniors fill many pleasant hours as round table discussions of books provide mental catalysts for thought-provoking conversations. Once the dust is swept out and the cobwebs eliminated from old, unused minds, wonderful things happen.

Even as a small boy, I remember listening for hours to my ninety-six-year-old great-grandmother tell about harrowing experiences her family had endured as they homesteaded a farm in the middle of Indian country in an isolated part of Idaho. If we could get Great-grandmother going, she was good for a lot of stories. Her wit and humor amazed our young minds. Her reminiscence of her early days when life was so different from our world kept us spellbound for hours. I have overheard discussions among seniors that rival any panel discussion I have ever participated in on a university level. Don't underestimate your mental abilities just because you may not have attended college. There is something about the wisdom accumulated by riding the earth around the sun a few dozen times that makes the puny knowledge and understanding of youth pale in comparison. More will be suggested later on how to use your wisdom to bless your family and acquaintances.

Old age does not need to be equated with loneliness and isolation. Until your mind makes you unaware that you are alone, you are able to develop social relationships. Two lonely people can easily make a happy duo. If necessary, a short ad in the newspaper or a public service announcement on the local radio or television station could generate the much-needed company. It is definitely true that seldom does anyone sense the responsibility to make something happen for us. If we expect someone to inconvenience themselves for us and they don't, we tend to get bitter and cynical about the world. However, if we expect absolutely nothing and someone does sacrifice for us, we are overwhelmed with feelings of appreciation.

While I am very much in favor of meeting the needs of individuals through welfare, I resent being forced to pay by an inefficient government.

If someone asked me to contribute to the needs of the elderly or poor, I would do it in a heartbeat and without any feelings of resentment. The same is true of service. When people serve us because they feel obligated, they send a silent message that they resent the time they spend with us. However, if we can help people voluntarily donate time and means to the cause of the elderly, both they and the elderly grow in respect and love for each other. Even though there may be organizations who shun the offered help of the elderly, there are many others who welcome your help. Acting as substitute grandparents for children born addicted to drugs or alcohol is a demanding but rewarding opportunity for service. With your love (which doesn't require a great deal of physical strength) a child can feel what immature or uncaring parents are unwilling to provide. If children grow up in an environment void of love, is it any wonder that they become a hostile element in society which in turn threatens our security?

My mother was well into her nineties and still flitted around like a woman half her age. She was about as selfless a person as I know. If she was not serving, she was not happy. She was sensitive to those who may not welcome her offers for help, but anyone who had tasted her homemade pies never withdrew the welcome mat when they saw her coming. See passed away just shy of her one-hundredth birthday.

Perhaps growing up a people watcher has made me more observant than many. I see some of Mom's friends who adopted the attitude that "the world owes them a living," and they seemed to shrivel up socially when their needs were not met. Mom seemed to be just the opposite. The more she forgot her own needs, the more radiant and fun to be around she grew. She continued to hold family dinners, host clubs, and take meals to the ill or those who had just had babies. She was always crocheting an afghan or tying a baby quilt, or working on a hundred other projects. We tried to get her to come and stay with us for a week or two, but it was rare when she would. She had too many things going. Too many people depended on her. Flowers needed watering, visits needed to be done, pies needed to be baked. The list was virtually endless.

The final area to be considered for taking dominion over your world during the twilight years is the spiritual. Perhaps now more than ever before, questions need to be asked and answers sought. For those who believe that life ends when death closes one's eyes, asking difficult questions about the next life may not have the same appeal. When physical strength disables you from sports or travel or even being out and about too much, it has a positive flip side. You are rewarded with additional time to ponder the real meaning of life. You may find that many of your friends will be more than anxious to discuss your thoughts about life after death.

There may be service you can render in your church or civic group. There are always those who need a listening ear or a shoulder to cry on. When we get outside ourselves in our quest to help others, the scope of our interest broadens and life becomes more meaningful. Quiet hours of thoughtful meditation often result in deeper insights into the real meaning of life. The rush of modern living renders it an almost impossibility to enjoy the silence. It requires real effort to exclude the detractors that rob us of that inner serenity that makes saints out of common people.

Is attitude toward growing old the main differentiating factor? If we could change our attitude, could we change the world? If the answer to those questions (in your own mind) is "yes," then don't you alone hold the key? What could possibly hold you back from controlling your own world, if you once determine you are going to change it?

Until twenty-five years ago when he died, I had a maternal uncle who was paraplegic from the time he was eighteen months old. He had contracted polio before there was any vaccine. Not to be denied his share of joy in life, he made those with far greater physical abilities look like wimps. He graduated from high school by being carried on people's backs from class to class. He later married my aunt (who was quadriplegic from polio). He supported his wife, played the guitar, was an artist, built a cabin, was on the city council, and then was the mayor of the city. He was active in civic and church affairs, and was a homespun philosopher. No one ever said, "Poor Clyde," after having been around him for five minutes. On the contrary, one would often leave his presence in a state of self-condemnation for being so weak when given so much.

During his last few years when his twisted spine and collapsing rib cage began to make breathing a full-time chore, he was the most active. I surmise that he realized his days were numbered. He did not want to leave life with a half a tank of gas. He finally collapsed, having given his best to the very end. He was not perfect. But he was an example of a gutsy person who would not allow the environment or the ill twists of life to deter him from enjoying life to the max. From his story and others like him, much of the logic and rationale of this book will come forth.

One of my wife's favorite sayings is, "God never gives us a wish without giving us the ability to achieve it." Maybe that is a little too cutesy, but maybe it is a profound truth. How disappointing it would be to arrive in eternity only to find that we had the power to create our own world in mortality and we shied away because we didn't believe in ourselves or our abilities.

Whether it be our physical, social, intellectual, or spiritual world, we are the only one who holds the key to determine the quality of existence we will enjoy during those final golden years. No matter where you are in the aging process or whatever habits you may have established, isn't now a good time to take control of your world and make things happen that will leave friends and family standing with mouths open as you exit on to the next exciting adventure in another dimension?

Chapter 2

BREAKING THE VICIOUS CYCLES

Do you remember as children getting into those verbal duels that had no end?

"You said I'm ugly!"

"Did not!"

"Did so!"

"Did not!"

"Did so!"

On and on it went until one or both of you tired and walked away from the silliness. Now with the reasoning ability seasoned by years of experience, we can see what we could not see then. No matter who won, you both lost. It is almost humorous, if it weren't so destructive, to listen to children and young adults engage in self-destructive attitudes and behaviors that can only result in heartache and disappointment if not corrected.

Unfortunately, bad habits and vicious cycles are not reserved for the young and inexperienced. Even many seniors can readily identify attitudes and personality traits that they know are less than ideal. Some excuse themselves by saying, "That's just the way I am!" as though lengthy, frequent use somehow legitimizes the undesirable characteristic. If it was wrong or less desirable when you were young, time hasn't changed anything.

At the very time in life when you have the most to give and want people around you for support, do you engage in behavior that has the opposite effect? One of my mother's friends was demanding, negative, and unappreciative to everyone who came to visit. She then complained to my mother that no one ever visited her, and when they did they seemed to be in a panic to get away as soon as possible. When confronted with a possible reason (her behavior toward them), she dismissed the thought with a defiant wave of the hand. My mother, being the kindly but firm woman that she was, stopped the verbal attack as soon as it started. Therefore, she was the one friend this elderly woman had. What a shame, because the small town where they both lived was very closely knit and the people were very willing to visit and help one another. Unless this woman admitted the cause of her isolation, it was likely to continue and perhaps get worse.

Other negative character traits seem to have developed in recent years. Seniors who have always been reserved and polished become crude and offensive. Some attribute the personality change to a mild stroke or the deterioration of the mind. However, those same people are selectively crude or offensive. When they choose to control their speech or behavior, because it is personally advantageous to do so, they are very much in control. It seems to be that when they see no need for self-control that they use whatever excuse is available to justify their bad manners.

Does age give license for bad manners or a lessening of self-control? You must answer that question for yourself. However, it seems evident that an artist or sculptor would do the fine tuning, the polish, the perfecting with the last strokes of the brush or the final blows with the chisel. If we intend to take our "masterpiece" (our personality) into eternity, why would we choose to mar it at the very last minute? It seems very counterproductive.

If you are up to the challenge, why not take a few minutes, stand back, and make a list of those attitudes, personality characteristics, relationships, and ways of doing things that you know you could improve? Don't get down on yourself. It may have taken many years to develop the bad habits. Give yourself plenty of time to correct them. Don't be in too big of a hurry. Change for the sake of change is dangerous. Often the end result is worse than the original state. Think each change through carefully. Create a vision in your mind about what the ideal would be. Drawing upon your long years of experience, consider those who have perfected the characteristic or trait you want to improve. Don't stop with one or two. Take enough time to get a broad-spectrum picture ranging from those who need some serious help in your chosen area of improvement all the way to those who have polished the trait to near perfection. You will likely not be on the very bottom (there are always those who are worse than we are). If you are honest, there will probably be those who are considerably better at a given behavior than we are.

Again, a word of caution. When you begin to realize how far you have to go in some areas and how many areas there are, the natural tendency is to get down on yourself. Going on a pity party is of absolutely no value. In fact, it is self-destructive. Refuse to tell yourself how bad you are. It just isn't true, and it isn't helpful.

If your shopping list of things you would like to change is fairly long, rank order them. That is, put the most important or pressing one first and then assign importance to each one, putting the ones of lesser importance near the bottom of the list. It may be that you will never get to the bottom of the list in this life. Not to worry, eternity has no end! If you are in the process of improving, it is hard to envision a God who would not allow you to continue until you have reached His mandated goal for us: "Be ye therefore **perfect**, even as your Father which is in heaven is perfect" (Matthew 5:48, emphasis added).

If your list is very short and yet people shy away from you, it might be helpful to find a trusted friend or relative and ask them to honestly critique you. Be very careful here. You are asking the imperfect to criticize to perfection the imperfect. While very often your relative or friend will be "dead on" in their analysis, they may also miss the boat by a mile. I am humored as I listen to the youth counsel each other on how to handle difficult social situations. Often, they have little or no basis for their advice since they have never successfully handled the problematic situation either. I read with total amazement a statement by a well-known marriage therapist: "I should be an expert in marriage and relationships; after all, I have been divorced four times!" If I wanted help securing my marriage, she would likely be the last person I would seek out for advice. I would probably travel to Nebraska and find a couple who have been successfully married for sixty or seventy years. They, not the divorced therapist, are the real experts.

Without becoming a burden on people by asking too many people and too often, it shouldn't be too difficult to get a reading on the areas that people who know and love you perceive you might do some fine tuning. If you receive some bad input, refuse to become upset. Consider the source and act accordingly. No matter what age we are, it is wise to take whatever criticism we receive from whatever source we receive it and run it through our mental filtering system. No matter if the person criticizing is higher or lower on the social ladder than we, no matter whether they are older or younger than we, no matter whether their intention for criticizing us is positive or negative, we will be wise to consider what they say. In the event that they are entirely off base (they accuse you of being totally selfish and you are not), you might profit by considering what you have done or said that gave the mistaken impression. Often friendships are destroyed over perceived differences. If we would open the lines of communication, we would soon discover that our differences, if they exist at all, are very minor. It might be as simple as the way you gesture while you talk that leads to the mistaken impression.

If the suggestions turn out not to be true and you can't discover anything you are doing to cause the mistaken impression, then you might consider that some people take pride in tearing other people down and putting them in their place. I would suspect that few of your close friends fall into this category. However, when you invite criticism, you must also be prepared to accept the good, positive comments along with the cruel, destructive criticism. If the cruel comments are entirely off base, you must have a "thick skin" and not take them too seriously.

For almost two decades I worked as a professional land surveyor. Too many times to count, I would be called in to mediate the settlement of an estate where land was involved. In one particularly touchy situation, two brothers and a sister (all in their sixties) were seated in a room with a very frustrated attorney. Dad had just passed away, and the children were trying to equitably divide the estate. The problematic situation had positioned itself years before. The children had disagreed with an initial land endowment of the (then living) mother and father. They had refused to speak to each other directly for the past ten years. Now both Mother and Father—their only verbal link to each other—had passed away. The attorney asked if I could open the lines of communication by acting as the mediator. All three of these people were more than twenty years my senior.

One brother said to me, "Would you tell my sister that I want a certain piece of ground because it is adjacent to my original gift?" The sister was sitting not ten feet from him!

I dutifully turned to the woman and said, "Your brother said he would like a certain piece of ground because it is adjacent his originally gifted property."

The woman said to me, "Would you tell my brother that I am unwilling to give that piece of property to him because it has sentimental value to me?"

I looked at the attorney, who rolled his eyes in an obvious gesture of frustration. After about half an hour of this childishness, I said to the three sixty-plus-year-old children, "These are the kinds of games my pre-adolescent children play. We can do this all night, or we can act like adults and become part of the solution and not part of the problem!" I figured they would attack me and have to get another surveyor to mediate the settlement.

To my surprise (and the near cardiac arrest of the attorney), they looked at each other and smiled. The oldest son broke the ice. "You know, Mr. Bott is right. We really are acting like children. Come on, you guys, we used to be the best of friends. What say we bury the hatchet and get back in the same family? You all know that was the dying wish of both Mom and Dad."

Tears flowed freely, embraces were exchanged, and the rest of the meeting was like a bit of heaven. I don't know if Mom and Dad could look in from the next life or not, but I'm sure if they could, they would have been very pleased. That was the only time that I offered to waive my fee, and the family insisted on paying me double the originally quoted price for settlement. Much more was settled that afternoon than an estate.

Do you have family, former friends, or acquaintances with whom fences need to be mended? Sometimes all it requires is for someone to be the bigger person and start the ball rolling. Even if the offense was real and intended, why would you give them power to control the level of happiness in your life? Hatred, hard feelings, bitterness, malice, envy, and so on all have a stifling effect on the level of inner peace and happiness we enjoy.

When my father (who died when I was only four and a half years old) was young, he had married a woman and had a son. The woman's mother had vowed to break up the marriage and eventually succeeded. My father subsequently married my mother and had five of us children before his death at age thirty-three. Through the years my paternal grandparents and my mother maintained almost radio silence about the half-brother that we had. He was never discussed and never included in any reunions or family vacations. In fact, I had never met him until about thirty years ago. A mutual acquaintance engineered a meeting. At first, I was hesitant to meet him. What would I say? We had nothing in common but a father who had abandoned him and died before I really became acquainted with him. He lived in the eastern United States and I lived in the West. He had children older than I am whom I had never met. The reasons for not meeting seemed compelling. At the insistence of my wife, I went to meet him. It was immediate friendship. After an hour of openly and freely conversing like old friends, he put his hand on my knee and said, "I have always wanted a brother. Now I have one!" The electricity was tangible in the room. There would have been a void in my life if I hadn't acquiesced to the demands of my wife and accepted the invitation of our mutual friend. He still lives in the East and I still live in the West. We don't see each other often, but we are friends and brothers. Scary, but not unexpected, we even look quite a bit alike.

Could either of those scenarios become part of your family or social condition? I share them, although they are personal and private, in hopes that someone will see themselves in the story and take the first steps toward reconciliation.

The world can be a very ugly place in which to live. Bad things happen to good people. Abuse may have occurred when you were younger. Scars are difficult to erase, and painful memories may be nearly impossible to forget. But those days are long gone. The abuser may be dead and buried. If they are still alive, they are likely so aged that they can't even get around. Whatever the case, why would you want to carry those hateful feelings in your eternal suitcase as you exit this life? Modern professionals suggest that it is necessary to go back and dredge up every nitty-gritty detail of every episode of abuse so you can deal with it and let it heal. From the number of marriages that have been ruined, families split apart, and friendships destroyed over this manner of "going through the healing process," I would suspect we ought to reevaluate the correctness of that premise. The Apostle Paul (who really was the abuser before his conversion) gave his formula for dealing with the ugly past. He said, "Brethren, I count not myself to have apprehended: but this one thing I do, forgetting those things which are behind, and reaching forth unto those things which are before" (Philippians 3:13).

Where bitterness may have cankered your soul, why not try letting God be the judge, jury, and executioner? Since He is a God of justice, no wrong will ever go unpunished, no good deed will ever go unrewarded. Of course, if there are legal implications, you are at liberty to seek redress. Once you have done all that the laws of man can do to remedy the situation, leave the rest in Divine hands and get on with your life. It is helpful to remember two things: 1) God could, if He chose, eliminate all wrongs, sufferings, and injustices. The fact that He chooses not to suggests that there may be Divine purpose in these trials. 2) Although we cannot always control what happens to us, we alone can determine what our reaction to the wrong will be. Trials are inherently neither good nor bad. They can either grind us down or polish us up. It depends on what you are made of.

Although modern experts suggest that the abused often become the abusers of the next generation, it does not have to be. I counseled with two women in California a number of years ago. Each had a similar story. They had been forced into an incestuous relationship with their fathers, which continued over a number of years. The first woman was bitter and resigned to a life void of meaning without the possibility of a genuine intimate relationship with a man. "After all," she said, "how could I have a normal life after what my father has done to me? He has completely ruined my life!"

The second victim took me off guard. She seemed so sweet and well adjusted. I asked her how she could possibly live a normal life after such terrible abuse she had suffered as a child. She responded, "I couldn't control what my father did to me during my childhood. He is truly a sick man. But why should I allow his sickness to ruin my life? I have a life to live and eternity to prepare for. Someday I hope someone can help him get his life in order. Until then, I'll just keep living my life and praying for him." The only difference I could detect between the two women was the attitude they took toward the offense and the offender.

Perhaps one more example of a vicious cycle that needed to be broken. I referred earlier in this chapter to my father. I'm sure he was a good man—I never really knew him—but he had developed and perfected a "Bott family trait." He was a sulker! His father had been a sulker. His grandfather had been a sulker. So on back, probably, to Adam Bott. You might say, "That is one of our family traits as well." However, the Botts seem to have mastered the art. My mother told me that Dad would go for two or three months without ever saying a word or answering a question. He would grunt and point if he wanted anything. Today we would probably diagnose him as being clinically depressed. Then, he was just sulking. After two or three months of his juvenile "silent treatment," he would one day snap out of it. Everyone was supposed to act as if nothing had happened. When asked what he was mad at, a common reply was, "I can't remember."

I knew from an early age that I either had those same genes or at least had a predisposition toward moodiness. Realizing the pain that my father's behavior had caused the family, I decided to break the cycle. It wasn't easy, but every time I would catch myself going quiet and starting to sulk, I would force myself to talk and seek out people I could associate with.

I realized that I had the power to control my mood when one day while sitting in the front room sulking (or at least being very quiet), the phone rang. My mom answered it and called out that it was for me. It didn't take five seconds to get from the couch to the phone, but in that five seconds I changed my attitude from a sullen, sulky, moody to a light, happy, enthused one. I answered the phone with a "Hi, what's going on?" In the course of five seconds I went from one end of the emotional continuum to the other, without the aid of any mind-altering drugs or psychotherapy.

Once I realized I could do it, I started to practice. Granted, perfect mood control did not happen overnight. Even to this day decades later, I have to watch to make sure I don't go too long without laughing and talking with people. But people listen in disbelief when I tell them about my sulky attitude.

Life really is your choice. No one can force you to harbor a certain attitude or act a certain way. If you have been abused and are currently acting out the role of abuser, get some help. Because of the challenges of life, we are not expected to "go it alone." Admit the wrongs you are doing, make it right with the abused, and subdue and take dominion over your world. The rewards are instantaneous. You will feel better about yourself. Others will feel more love and kindness toward you. Even if they are hesitant to forgive you, you will have done everything in your power to fix the situation. At first people may view your resolve to break these vicious cycles with suspicion. They may view your efforts to change as a temporary fad. As you continue, you'll find added strength that will encourage you to take on additional challenges. Life changes and self-improvement almost become like a game. It is fun to watch an "old dog learn new tricks."

If no one ever acknowledges your efforts to change and break vicious cycles, there will be an inner peace because you'll sense that you are coming closer to the God-given commandment to be perfect than you have ever been. For the few detractors who will ridicule you and try to pull you back, you will develop a greater sense of empathy and sympathy. This new-found mercy you develop for others will automatically lead you to the subject of the next chapter. Isn't today a good day to start breaking vicious cycles that you have inherited from generations now past?

Chapter 3

OVERLOOKING PERSONAL DIFFERENCES FOR A HIGHER CAUSE

It seems like most of the principles discussed in this book come from dumb mistakes I have made over a lifetime. As a young man growing up in a small rural town, I had a group of rowdy friends who always did things together. During the summer months when school was not in session, we would spend many hours at the swimming hole in the river just below our home. As with all kids, we had our times when one or more of us were at odds with the group. On this particular day two of my friends had come to my house intent on going swimming. We had engaged in a heated argument. Words were said, cutting remarks made, and the two "former" friends departed for the river without me. I would never speak to them again!

As I sat in the back yard concocting plans of retaliation, I heard a desperate cry for help. Realizing my "former" friends were in trouble, my first inclination was to let them drown. In an instant I was on my feet and running at top speed toward the swimming hole. I hurdled fences, jumped irrigation ditches, broke through the willows, and arrived at the swimming hole to see my friend frantically diving for my other friend, who had become lodged in some submerged driftwood and couldn't surface. In a combined frantic effort, we freed him and with a little effort he was resuscitated. We lay on the bank of the river, exhausted from the exertion. With tears in his eyes (something which tough young boys never have), my friend thanked me for saving his life.

To this day I do not remember what we disagreed over or why I was so angry at them. I do remember the feelings of love we felt for each other. Over a lifetime we have remained good friends. Although we had more arguments in the years that followed, our friendship was never again in question.

As I have tried to evaluate the situation, I have determined that there was a higher cause (saving my friend's life) that superseded my hurt feelings. Had I hesitated in making the decision and argued with myself for just another few seconds, it would probably have been too late to save my friend.

How is it in your life? Is there a "higher cause" that needs to be given top priority before there are devastating, irreversible results? The power, wisdom, and potential for good that a grandma or grandpa have on the grandchildren seems to be a higher cause than the petty differences (real or perceived) between parents and children. Some adult children take a childish approach to problems with their parents. "We'll show them! We just won't let them associate with our children!" Whenever we use people as pawns on the chessboard of life, we make a terrible mistake. What would be the results of going to your son or daughter and apologizing for the hard feelings that exist?

Note carefully, I did not say apologize for being in the wrong. You may not be in the wrong at all. But are you not genuinely sorry for the hard feelings that exist? I have never been an advocate of taking the blame for something someone else did. But I can apologize all day long without feeling like I am betraying my sense of justice, for the negative feelings that are generated by the differences.

Too many older couples have developed barriers of ice between husband and wife. Failing to learn how to resolve differences has resulted in an epidemic of bickering and reciprocating cuts and slams. As a result, very sensitive grandchildren either shy away from visiting grandparents or (even worse) learn from their bad example habits that will perpetuate for another generation the sorrow-producing practices of childish arguing. Isn't there a higher cause? Wouldn't it be to the eternal advantage of everyone involved if the grandparents agreed to set aside their differences whenever the children bring the grandchildren by for a visit?

A caution needs to be mentioned. Children are really good at seeing through a facade. If you are just faking a good relationship, they will detect (what they call) the hypocrisy of the grandparents. So, what can be done? If you do not enjoy the hard feelings generated when you disagree, fight, and argue with your spouse, why not call a truce and sit down and devise a plan to eliminate the problem? Not everyone in the world argues and fights. Find out from them how they do it.

Perhaps without going into great detail, we could discuss a couple of principles that have helped eliminate fights and arguments in our marriage. First, choose the time to attack differences and problems when neither of you are tired, sick, or grouchy. If you say there isn't a time like that, you are probably not being as perceptive as you'll need to be. Usually (especially if you are both retired) mid-morning after a good breakfast or in the afternoon after a refreshing nap would be a good time. It is helpful to have a regularly scheduled time to resolve your differences. Many couples find that going on a walk or a ride in the car makes it easier to talk things through. Rather than focusing on the negative or things you need to "fix" first, start with telling each other what is going well in your marriage. One of the sobering facts of life seems to be that we see exactly what we look for. If you look for the flaws and weaknesses, you will probably find them whether or not they are there.

My wife has about given up on sending me to the grocery store. I'm not a great shopper. Don't misunderstand, I am deadly accurate in getting exactly what she sends me for. However, when I get home, she'll ask, "What were the advertised specials?" I have absolutely no idea. It wasn't on the list and I didn't look for them! Realizing that I find what I look for, it pays big dividends not to scrutinize too closely the flaws in my wife. If she used the same microscopic approach to looking for my weaknesses, we wouldn't have enough gas in the tank to work through all our differences.

When I know that each of our problem-solving sessions will begin with a time of pointing out the positive aspects of our relationship, I automatically start to look for them. Not surprisingly, I find a lot to be thankful for because that is what I am looking for. Do yourself a favor and take time each day looking for what is right in your relationship, rather than focusing solely on what is wrong and needs fixing.

The next suggestion is to limit your suggestions for areas that need attention to two or three. If my wife brought a whole shopping list of things I need to improve on to the discussion, I may become discouraged and mistakenly believe that I must be totally no good. Since she has the rest of my life to fine tune and polish me, if she is patient over the years she'll get a chance to draw my attention to the majority of things she would like me to correct. If each one will come to the corrective session with the attitude that "we have a really good marriage and we can make it better by doing the following things," you will be surprised how much fun working together can be.

One absolute imperative: *Focus on the problem and not on the person.* Although it is I who leaves my socks in a heap at the bottom of the bed, my wife will say, "I think we could eliminate some hard feelings if we didn't leave our clothes lying around the house." I know exactly what she is talking about and who the offender is. But she does not attack me, and I don't attack her—that would be an argument. If we insist on attacking the issue and not the person, you will discover (pleasantly) that the result is the same (the socks are picked up), but the feelings are far different from when you attack the person for his behavior.

That point is so important that I want to emphasize it again. Attack the issue (attitude, behavior, conduct) and not the person. It is the dirty dishes in the sink, not the wife who leaves the dirty dishes in the sink. It is the seat on the toilet left up, not the husband who leaves the seat on the toilet up. It is the lights that are left on all night, not the wife who leaves the lights on all night. As a teacher/counselor all of my adult life, I have discovered that the couples who exhibit the most love and unity in their marriages are those who differentiate between the behavior and the person. Be perceptive enough to see: "I love the person. I dislike the behavior."

After identifying the issues you want to work on, try to agree on a solution to the problem. Again, from my counseling background, I have observed that most people do not separate in their minds the problem from the solution. Too many people think they are solving the issue when they are only rehashing the problem. Clearly establish in your mind the difference between the problem and the solution. Problems can be identified and quantified in a very short time. Solutions may take more time.

Try to avoid mandating a solution. "It must be done my way" usually meets with resistance. When there is agreement between the disagreeing parties on how to solve a problem, almost any solution will work. One of the truly great revelations in my hard-hearted, always right youth was to realize that other people could have good ideas too. Surprisingly, many of their proposed solutions were actually better than mine. It does require some humility to admit that my ideas are not always the best. Especially in dealing with children, you might bite your tongue more often than you'd like as they grow into fatherhood or motherhood. If one or both of your parents constantly butted in on your parenting, you probably resented it. Do not perpetuate the problems of the past into the next generation.

Consider as many possible solutions as you can. Be creative. Don't mock or make fun of, or discard as stupid any idea or possible solution. Consider each one. Some of the proposed solutions will be stupid and can't be taken seriously. After each of you have had a chance to propose all the possible solutions you can think of, discuss the merits of each until you both are sure you understand what the other partner means by the proposed solution they presented. After you understand each option, try to agree on which one you will choose. Be willing to give and take. If we choose your option this week, we may choose my suggestion next week.

Set a time when you can account. It could be each evening at the dinner table, once a week on Sunday, every night before you go to bed—any time you agree on is all right. If you don't follow through and provide a time to account, your new resolve will rapidly dwindle and disappear. Sometimes a note on the fridge reminding of the commitment will help.

Since it has taken a lifetime to develop the habits you are trying to break, be a bit flexible when mistakes are made. Habits are difficult to break. Expect a few setbacks. But if you will work together, the bad habits that may cause your children and grandchildren to shy away from you will rapidly disappear.

Many seniors play life like it is a game. Lawsuits are filed not necessarily because wrongs have been committed but because it fills up the empty hours and gives everyone something to talk about. Rumors and gossip may be spread just to see what happens. Without a focus for life, it is easy to start brush fires so we can see the flames and smoke only to find that our homes are consumed by the flames as the fire gets out of control.

A more focused approach might be to improve everyone you touch. Gossip destroys those who are the subjects and those who are the perpetrators. It is a habit that seems to be as addicting as drugs are to the youth of today. Breaking the gossip habit will take effort and constant vigilance, but it can happen.

There is no real benefit in believing a false report. It is like building a high-rise on a foundation of sand. There is only one legitimate way to know if something is true or not—ask. From my surveying experience and from my extended counseling experience, much of the heartache and sorrow we endure could be reduced, if not eliminated all together, by simply asking for the facts from a person who knows—the individual in question. If the habit of gossip is ingrained deeply into your character, prepare yourself for a battle. For many people it is an unconscious response. Perhaps part of the "hell" people will suffer will be seeing the ripple effect of suffering caused by our careless spreading of unsubstantiated information.

Someone impressed a little saying upon me years ago that helps me control my tongue. Ask yourself three questions before passing anything on: 1) Is it true? 2) Is it kind? 3) Is it necessary? Misinformation has been the kindling agent for wars within families, neighborhoods, countries, and the world. In the very time of life when you have the greatest potential to be a peacemaker, don't fall prey to the easy path of sowing discord and hatred by the things you say. The world is in dire need of healers rather than destroyers. If you want to distinguish yourself above the crowd, speak things that promote peace rather than divisiveness.

If you want to see how deeply ingrained negativism is in your group, try saying only good things about people. If it is a serious problem, the people you speak to will look at you with that "what's wrong with you?" look. Those wallowing in the negative are usually not overly excited about hearing positive, good things.

If there is a higher cause in the social interactions of people, it will have to be fostered by those who refuse to become part of the doomsayers. Too many people are expert at pointing out the problems of society. Precious few have any workable, constructive suggestions on how to fix the problems. In the company where I was part owner, we had a policy that every criticism must be accompanied by at least one possible solution. In social settings when people begin to complain about how tough life is or how bad they have it, I sometimes say, "You've done a great job identifying the problem. What do you intend to do about it?" It is almost laughable to see their startled response. Why complain if we aren't going to fix it?

Everyone from the "armchair quarterback" to the talk show host who majors in exposing the dirty linen of the leaders of the nation has perfected the ability to confess the other guy's sins. Sure, it is easy to get down on the local sports team for going through a slump or experiencing a losing streak. It is more challenging to put on the suit and turn things around. The greatest self-proclaimed experts I have seen in marriage and family counseling are those who are single and have no children. When we are young, we know all of the answers. When we get older, we realize we don't even know all of the questions. Our "pat answers" are not always so "pat." Simplistic answers to complex problems are a dime a dozen and seldom work. Just because something is written in a textbook does not mean it's necessarily workable.

From your vantage point of years of experience, you can recognize those solutions that work and those that don't, although they may sound good on paper. I'm not sure there is a good substitute for age and experience. Those of us who have rowed most of the way across the lake of life are smart enough to know that when the boat is leaking and sinking there is no time to argue over who punched a hole in the hull. If we want to stay afloat as a society, family, or couple, we'd better spend our precious time and resources bailing out the water. There will be time when we arrive at the shore to assess fault and blame if we are even inclined to at that point. But for right now, we have work to do.

Is there a higher cause? I have only mentioned a few areas where misdirected emphasis contributes to the pain and suffering of families and society. As you think about other areas of your life, you may readily discover that a higher cause impels you to abandon petty, small grievances and to run to the swimming hole to make the rescue. By merely looking beyond our own self-centered needs, it becomes painfully apparent that the demand on our time and energy goes beyond what we can muster if we are willing to forget ourselves into immortal glory.

Don't underestimate the impact you can have. You are only one, but you are one. Perhaps you can't be everything to everybody, but you can be something to somebody. What you can do, you ought to do. And with the help of the Almighty, what you ought to do, you will do. One determined individual can change an entire nation—either for good or ill. Using the snowballing effect, you start with yourself, gather around you your family and friends, and eventually end up changing the world. Consider the impact of Mother Teresa. Consider the impact of Adolf Hitler. Both were individuals. Both had only twenty-four hours in a day. Both had only one life to live. The net result of their impact will endure long after they have gone to their eternal reward or punishment.

It may take some time, but with effort and determination you can make things happen. When the stumbling blocks of life are viewed as stepping-stones to greater heights, there isn't anything you can't accomplish. I really like a statement attributed to Joan of Arc at the time of her martyrdom. She said: "The world can use these words. I know this now—every man gives his life for what he believes; every woman gives her life for what she believes. Sometime people believe in little or nothing, and yet they give their lives to that little or nothing. One life is all we have, and we live it as we believe in living it, and then it's gone. But to surrender what you are and live without belief is more terrible than dying, even more terrible than dying young."[1]

That is a pretty mature response for a nineteen-year-old maid about to be burned at the stake. Whether we improve the world by leaving it a better place, or whether we leave sorrow and misery in our wake, there is one thing for sure: we are one day closer to death today than we were yesterday. Someday we will die. All we take with us are the experiences we have had. Why not take a suitcase full of good memories? Is there a higher cause?

---

1. Sterling W. Sill, *The Majesty of Books*, quoted in *Out of the Best Books* (Salt Lake City: Deseret Book), 243.

Chapter 4

MODELING PATIENCE

Progression through life seems to follow a bell-shaped curve for some. Infants start out with no ability to take care of themselves. They are totally reliant on others for even their basic needs for continued existence. Within a few months they learn that crying and fussing causes their caretakers to scramble to diagnose and meet their needs. As they mature, they are expected to meet more of their own needs. Then crying is viewed as a lack of patience or even as a temper tantrum. For the majority of our lives we are expected to take care of our own needs. There even comes a point when we are expected to suppress our own wants and desires in order to help meet the needs of others. Some people, as they near the end of life, are required by circumstance (either mental, physical, or both both) to rely almost entirely on others for their basic needs. After having been independent for so many years it is frustrating to be obliged to rely on others. Hopefully, as we approach that time, we will not regress in our patience level to the demanding level of infancy.

Watching the evening news can be depressing. Stories of the inhumanity of man to man are a daily diet on which the media feeds us. To listen to newscasters, one would believe that the entire world has lost its sanity. Perhaps it has, but I sure meet a lot of good, solid people as I travel the world. It is alarming to read of motorists gunning down or ramming another motorist who cut them off on the freeway. The stories of young people shooting each other over a few ill-spoken words leaves us wondering if patience failed to mature as their bodies matured.

Unfortunately, violence within families seems to be escalating. Spouse abuse is common. Child abuse receives almost daily attention in the media. It almost seems that perfection is expected of "the other guy," but tolerance is expected when I fall short. What can you do to stem the senseless tide of violence fueled by a total lack of patience? You may think the answer to that question is "nothing." Upon a little closer scrutiny there is a great deal we can do. Some things we can do directly; others things will require more patience as we quietly influence others.

On the highways we watch as youthful drivers (and some not so youthful) dart between cars, changing lanes frequently, endangering everyone's lives in order to get ahead. On the way to work, I encountered one such young man. I first saw him when I looked in my rearview mirror and noticed that he was almost driving in my back seat. I was in the slow lane, and there were cars in front of me so there wasn't much I could do. As soon as there was the smallest break in the cars in the adjacent lane, he darted over. Impatiently he sounded his horn at the car in front of him. Not wanting to cause an accident, I slowed a little to let the car in front of this young driver move into my lane and let him pass. The exchange was made and the young man raced forward a whole car length! There was a slight space between the car in front of me and the next one forward. The reckless young man's car darted forward. I decided to see how much his changing lanes and endangering everyone else on the highway would net him. We had about four miles to drive before I left the highway to enter the campus. He continued his erratic behavior of lane changing for the entire distance. When I turned into the left-turn lane to enter the campus, you can probably guess who was revving his engine waiting for the light to change in the lane immediately to my right. He had not gained a single car length in that four-mile stretch.

One area where you and I can make an immediate, significant difference is on the highways. A little patience could prevent a lot of accidents and maybe even decrease the death toll through senseless shooting and ramming. Waiting for a pedestrian to cross even after the light has turned green is an example the youth could stand to see. Perhaps in those and many other observable areas, we could model what patience is like.

It is too bad that many of today's youth seem to feel like they must live their lives entirely in the fast lane. Unfortunately, an unprecedented number are driving in the fast lane only to find that others exhibit the same intolerance they have. The combination is explosive and deadly.

One of the values of growing older is our inability to do everything *right now.* Impetuosity seems to be more an earmark of youth than of the mature. I used to become really frustrated with my grandfather when he would sit for hours (at least it seemed like hours to me) and figure out how to do a project. He used to say, "Hold your horses." As time passed, I began to appreciate that his time spent thinking the problem through was well rewarded by doing the job quicker and with less effort than if we had just plowed into the project. Now I catch myself saying to my children and grandchildren, "Hold your horses."

In many young families the parents yell at and berate the children who cannot perform simple tasks as easily and efficiently as their parents. Your patience in helping grandchildren or young neighbor children learn how to do tasks without the fear of being yelled at could be a saving factor in their young lives. Many of today's youth refuse to try when failure is a likely outcome because of their fear of parental reprisal. Good thing for us Thomas Edison's mother and father were not impatient, yelling parents. We may still be sitting in the dark!

It may even be a little irritating to your children to remind them of years gone by when they were learning to perform complex tasks. A good memory is one of the keys to good parenting. If you have just learned recently not to yell and berate, you might remind them how much they hated being yelled at and how much you regret having done it. If you were the patient kind, remind them that you were more tolerant with them than they are being with their children.

As the body gets older and more subject to disease and injury, it requires more patience on our part to take extra precautions. Even when we are as careful as we can be, there are still times when our health fails and we have some down time. Graciously accepting our plight without complaint and patiently enduring the rough spots in our road of life can have a silent but profound effect on the lives of our children and grandchildren as they view our example.

Earlier in the book I mentioned my uncle who was paralyzed from polio during his youth. I remember complaining to him one day when I had turned my ankle while playing football. He let me rant and rave for awhile about how unfair it was to miss out on the next high school football game. He nodded understandingly until it finally dawned on me that he hadn't walked for decades and wouldn't for the rest of his life. My injury would soon heal and I would be running and playing again. He never would. What a silent lesson he taught me.

Frustration levels seem to be spiraling with each passing day. Unfortunately for the recipient, the minor infraction that brings on the abuse (either verbal or physical) is usually only the final straw. The accumulation of pent-up frustrations is a disaster waiting to happen. Over the years you have, of necessity, learned to release some of the pent-up frustrations. It is impossible to accumulate a lifetime of frustration and still remain sane and balanced. Take a few minutes and see if you can verbalize your technique. Talk to a few of your senior friends and see how they "unwind." Then in a less highly charged situation, share the wisdom of the aged with your children and grandchildren.

When the situations arise in the future in their lives (and they will arise), your words may echo in their minds. Your counsel may give them the needed ammunition to blow away the frustrations without losing their temper. You could adopt the attitude: "Let them learn it the hard way as we did." They will probably learn as you did. The problem is that our society is so much more violent than it was in our day that they may learn either from a prison cell or from the next life. Life is just not long enough to make all the mistakes of the preceding generations. What a gift we can give to those who follow us. Share with them what works and what doesn't work. Even if you didn't learn your lessons easily (you suffered a painful divorce or lost a child from the family through rebellion), your recital of what you did wrong or what you should have done differently could make all the difference in the world in your children's lives.

Because we live in an information-based world, don't be surprised if your children become irritated at you for sharing your story. After all, they do know so much more than we do! The amount of knowledge may have exploded, but the principles behind happiness and successful living have not changed. Learning to live together in love and harmony is as difficult now as it was when we were young. It was no easier then and likely, it will be no easier in a hundred years from now. For as smart as human beings are, we still haven't been able to find a simple set of rules to avoid war on every level from the couple to the family to the world.

In some ways you can use your example of overcoming problems to demonstrate that mastery is possible. If you were an abuser earlier in life, the whole world would be interested in how you broke out of the habit. If you were addicted to alcohol or tobacco in your youth but have overcome the addiction, millions would like to know how you did it. If you had an extremely short fuse on your violent temper when you were younger but have since developed a greater degree of patience, billions would be interested in how you successfully conquered the problem.

The story is told of a jealous courtier who attended a banquet held in honor of Columbus. The courtier asked Columbus, in an attempt to embarrass him, if he did not think someone else would have discovered America if he hadn't. Columbus did not respond directly but posed a challenge to those gathered around the table. He asked each one to take an egg and stand it on end. After everyone had tried with no success until the frustration level was rising, Columbus took his egg and struck one end on the table so the one end broke. He then left it standing on the broken part. After he had shown how to do it, everyone was able to follow. So it is with the great challenges of life. Whenever we can find someone to show us how to do the impossible, the impossible not only becomes doable but relatively easy. I can still see in my mind's eye the vision of the gnarled, arthritic hands of my aged grandmother, guiding my little sister's hands as she taught her to crochet. All of the verbal instructions in the world could not replace the skillful maneuvering of expert hands who knew the ropes.

Not everyone will learn by being taught. Some seem destined to learn by sad experience. We can be comforted to know that the lessons of life will be learned either by being taught or by sad experience, but they will be learned. In suggesting that you model how to succeed for your children and grandchildren, I am not suggesting that you infringe on their agency. They always have the freedom to "suffer" if they choose. It is when they seem to have no other option than failure because they haven't been taught that we should feel ashamed.

Part of the art of modeling patience is to be patient when people reject our help. To stand back and let the inescapable consequences follow poor choices is not easy to do. Of course, we love our children and grandchildren and do not want to see them suffer. However, it would be very short-sighted to protect them from the natural consequences of their actions. A poor investment engaged in against your counsel would be better left to run its course than to rescue your loved one from the financial hurt that will follow. How will they learn if you continually "rescue" them? Was there someone who always "rescued" you? I would doubt there was. Life just doesn't seem to be designed that way. How many times does God step in and "rescue" His children from poor choices, even though they may be life-threatening?

You may even suffer some criticism for not coming to the rescue. Again, your ability to model patience when you are under verbal attack provides a great example for those who desperately need to learn patience before society decides they will not tolerate childish temper tantrums and finds a secure place to lock them away.

We live in a "get-rich-quick" world. Almost weekly we receive advertisements in the mail informing us that we have made the first, second, or third cuts on a multi-million-dollar sweepstakes. The lottery in many states represent the same mentality—something for nothing. It is alarming to see employees in the service sector of society who are not service oriented. Somehow the waitress in a restaurant gives the impression she is doing you a favor in waiting on you. The checker at the grocery store becomes irritated if you don't do everything just right. The whole world could use a dose of "earning your living by the sweat of your face" philosophy (see Genesis 3:19).

While it is true that a precious few are enriched by winning the lottery or the sweepstakes, it is painfully evident that millions of people pay and never win anything. A young "wanna be" approached Liberace after a stirring concert and said, "I'd give anything to play like you!"

Liberace reportedly said, "Would you give everything to play like I do?"

The young man answered, "Yes."

"Good," said Liberace, "because that is exactly what it cost me to play like this—everything."

Everything from patience in taking college courses to get a degree, becoming proficient in the use of the computer, learning to drive a car safely, or mastering a musical instrument requires time and effort. Without the patience you can model for them, many will become frustrated and quit in despair long before the desired goal is achieved.

The power of example cannot be overstated. It is easy to read about the patience and effort needed to endure to the end. It is much more encouraging to watch someone you love and admire actually enduring to the end. Does life have to be easy? Does perseverance pay off? Can one patiently work through the challenges of life without becoming a mental basket case? The resounding answer to each of these questions is "yes." The way seems much more achievable when I have a model to follow. Why not be that model?

Chapter 5

CAPITALIZING ON THE WISDOM OF THE AGED

Some things just take time. You cannot force a fruit to ripen faster than the genetic time clock within. How many times have you looked back on your life and said something like, "If I had only known then what I know now, I could have been so much better as a mother or father!" What you have stated is a fact of life. It seems about the time all of our children are married and have left home, we begin to understand how to be effective parents. That is probably why we have grandparents and senior citizens!

Each generation seems destined to learn that "old-fashioned" does not connote inferiority or non-desirability. This generation has decided that morality is old-fashioned. They are also having to cope with AIDS and other sexually transmitted diseases that defy the wisdom of modern man to cure. However, the cure is so simple for those of our generation. It doesn't require billions of dollars in research, hundreds of programs in classrooms as young as elementary grades teaching children how to have "safe sex," or national councils who wring their hands on how to curb illicit drug use. All it would take is a return to the wisdom of the aged—live moral, chaste lives. However, how many times in recent years have you heard that as a suggested solution?

In absolutely every aspect of our lives, there are lessons learned through experience that could greatly benefit the rising generation. Recently I stood in a line at the bank waiting for the next available teller. There were several people in front of me. One was a middle-aged woman who dressed, talked, and acted like a business executive. Immediately in front of her was a teenage boy who was doing everything in his power to make a statement. His hair was about half an inch long and had been dyed bright pink. He had half a dozen earrings in each ear. He had pierced his eyebrow and his nose, and his lip and had a gold chain linking each one. His clothes, as well as his appearance, were revolting to those around him. As he approached the bank teller, he asked where he could apply for a job. I'm sure there is some federal regulation somewhere that prohibits discriminating for a job based on personal appearance, but the government would have an impossible time enforcing it. The teller looked at him and said, "The bank isn't hiring anyone right now." The young man made some off-handed comment and walked out. I listened as the female executive and the teller exchanged expressions of disbelief at the boy's appearance and reaffirmed that even if there were a hundred openings, he would not be considered.

Being an educator, I took a different approach. I asked myself, "How can I help the young man know that his 'statement' is going to cost him years of heartache and rejection because corporate America is not willing to look beyond the exterior and see what is really in his head and his heart?" I wonder who could get the attention of the young man to help him know how other people perceived him.

I would not be surprised if the boy's parents have tried to reason with him many times. Likely he would reject their efforts and accuse them of being more concerned about the impression their societal friends might get above their love for him. I have heard that line of reasoning for the last four decades as a teacher. Because of my experience, I am convinced that grandparents or other respected seniors can often have a greater impact than parents on the rising generation during those turbulent teenage years.

Could you invite the boy to help you with some yard work? Then during a casual conversation, could you share with him an example or story from your past that might plant a seed that may not germinate for some time, that there is a connection between his rejection and his appearance? It need not be (in fact, should not be) in the form of lecturing or preaching. He is already accustomed to turning his mind off whenever he senses another lecture. Young people still like stories, especially those they can identify with in principle.

You may not even have a story that is factual to tell. As I read the parables in the New Testament, I wonder how many parables are stories that actually happened or if they were real enough that they could have happened. For example, was there really a man on the road to Jericho? Whether there was or wasn't isn't nearly as significant as the fact that the Savior got a lot of good miles out of the example. Could there be a similar experience (a "road to Jericho" example) you could use to help the boy learn a lesson?

It doesn't matter whether you have a college degree—you have lived 365 days a year times the number of years you have been alive. The longer you've lived, the more time you have had to observe life. Your ability to relate the present to the past will increase as you consciously look for parallels. You need not worry if the young person you are talking to sees your "parable" as incredible; they will let you know. The rolling of the eyes is one example. Simple words or phrases like "Right," "Get a life," "Sure," and "Really!" all communicate the youth's rejection or at least serious questioning of the relevance of your example. With a little practice you can learn how to package your instructions so that rejection is rare.

A word of caution in working with the young: refrain from using such phrases as "when I was your age" or "in my day" or "you kids never would have survived if you had lived when I was young." Although it is true that many kids are now more play-oriented than work-oriented, it is also true that there are not as many farms to work on or jobs that need to be done (chopping wood, hauling water, feeding the chickens, slopping the hogs, and so on) as there were in our day. We can hardly be justified in criticizing them for not doing something that is not available to them.

You will also quickly discover that the youth may have a shorter attention span than you remember having. You may never have even considered walking away from an adult when they were speaking to you. Kids do that all the time today. Don't be frustrated. If you refuse to superimpose your standards, you will be more successful in helping them. Spend a little time listening to them. Ask questions and do a little research with those who work daily with the youth. You will find out what their world is really like. It may shock you, but you will at least be conversant with their situation and can tailor your instruction to meet their needs.

Although I have talked directly about youth, the same is probably true for your children. They too have grown up in a different world. The difference between your children and your grandchildren, however, is that you were forced by your relationship to your children to be part of their world. However, listening to your children or other adults in the same age group will ensure that you are not perceived as "old-fashioned" and "out of touch." There is a certain "with-it-ness" that makes older people appealing to the younger ones.

Another word of caution: be careful in trying to adopt their manner of speech. The words they say may not have the same meaning to them as they did to you. For example, even when I was young, we would say in response to a question about how a date went, "Oh, we had a gay old time," meaning, of course, that we had a really good time. If you were to say that today, it would have an entirely different meaning. Because "gay" is now associated with homosexual, we would be looked at with disdain. When my children and students use language that I am not sure I understand, I ask. You will be surprised to learn that often they do not understand the exact meaning of a term or phrase they use. They also may not understand words or terms that you use.

If they sense that you are trying too hard to be part of their world, it may turn them off. It is better to use language you are sure you know the meaning of and let them translate it into their own language. The next point is equally as frustrating. Decades ago the government decided to eliminate discrimination based on race—a good move. However, as the government usually does, they tried to legislate equality, which will never happen. Since entrance exams to gain admittance to the universities favored those whose backgrounds included educated parents, something had to be done because too many minorities were excluded from universities. So, rather than intensify the pre-college learning of the minorities, the government mandated lowering the entrance requirements. Sound like a good idea? Not exactly.

Ever since that time, nationally funded reports such as "Nation at Risk" have raised the warning flags that our whole educational system is on the brink of collapse. So, what is my point? Where less has been expected, less has been accomplished. The language you and I take for granted as elementary and understood by everyone who speaks English may be totally unfamiliar to the youth of today. It is not that they are not intelligent—many of them make us look like dummies. They just haven't been required to bite the bullet and learn the language.

In our home I consciously tried to use language familiar to college-level students and even terminology used in my doctoral program. We tried to teach our children to ask if they do not understand the words we use. One day I used a rather "highfalutin" word (recalcitrant) to describe our teenage son's attitude. He looked at me and asked, "Dad, was that a compliment or a cut?" We laughed together. Then I wrote the word on a piece of paper and told him to go look it up. He came back in a few minutes with a rather exultant attitude. He quoted: "Recalcitrant—obstinately defiant of authority or restraint." Then he said, "Dad, that wasn't a compliment! What does *obstinately* mean?" This time he was teasing and we both laughed again.

Do not stand aghast at their lack of understanding of the most basic words in our language. They could back you against the wall at any time by having you try to define the language common to them. Sometimes, if I see that unsure look in their countenance, I will ask them to tell me what I just told them. It is simple to detect a lack of understanding from their erroneous recital. Somehow, in order to effectively help other people, we must communicate. Don't overestimate their ability to understand you.

Wisdom goes far beyond the use of language. How to solve differences without fighting is one of the challenges of the very young. If we could share with our grandchildren and other young children the art of compromising, negotiating, and communicating, we would be doing the world a tremendous (and absolutely essential) favor. Youth wouldn't be killing and injuring youth at an unprecedented rate if they had learned how to peacefully resolve differences. Who better than those who have lived through a world war and many other major conflicts to teach that "might doesn't make right"?

Sulking and temper tantrums seem common even among adolescents and adults. Yet your longevity should have enabled you to see that both temper tantrums and sulking are lose–lose situations.

Nobody wins when those tactics are employed. Even a win–lose situation is not desirable. With a little effort, almost every social interaction can be turned into a win–win situation. It will require thought and diplomacy to show youth and adults how to avoid any "lose" experiences. For example, if you have either suffered through a painful divorce yourself or have witnessed the long-term, negative ripple effects of divorce in the lives of others, you can readily testify that divorce really is a lose–lose proposition. From your vantage point, it is easier and much more effective to try to intervene in the lives of those who believe that divorce is a quick fix to all of their problems. Even divorce counselors are questioning whether the negative after-effects of divorce are more damaging than staying in a less-than-ideal marriage and trying to work out the differences.

Along with the get-rich-quick schemes that are impoverishing so many people is another trick used by those who care nothing about the individual and his happiness. I refer to the "easy credit" trap. Plastic money is made to sound so good that the unsuspecting find themselves drowning in credit-card payments with no possible way of getting out. Escalating bankruptcies should raise a warning flag to the unwary. Over the years you have lived long enough to see the paper-thin facade of "something for nothing." The "buy now and pay later" philosophy puts the entire emphasis on the immediate satisfaction of having something calculated to make us happy, but totally ignores the "pay later" hook. At between 18 percent and 21 percent or even higher interest rates, the "good deal" that was so simple to attain becomes a millstone about the neck of so many young married couples.

You may have noticed that young couples "need" everything their parents have. Someone must help them see the difference between a want and a need. In many of their young minds, the luxuries of life are viewed as absolute necessities. Someone who has ridden the earth around the sun a few dozen more times than they have needs to draw upon their wisdom to teach the young that the greatest *things* in life are not *things* but relationships. Things do not make us happy. When we look to temporary, perishable things to bring lasting happiness and satisfaction, we are looking for that which will never happen. Only those who have lived a lifetime know for sure the truth of that statement. As I have taken the time to study the lives of some of the richest men and women in the world, it became shockingly apparent that worldly wealth did not bring happiness and very often was very short-lived. No matter how much money greedy people make, it isn't quite enough. When the focus is on family, friends, and relationships, you still have a firm base of support even if you suffer financial reverses.

Perhaps the next area of focus is one the world would scorn as ridiculous but those who have lived long enough can bear ample testimony of its truthfulness. I am referring to physical over-indulgence. When we were young it seems that we could eat anything we wanted and our metabolic rate was sufficient to burn off what we didn't need. There seemed to be a magical point in life (near forty for many) when the metabolic rate slows down and the extra pounds accumulate rather than dissipate. Although there is a great emphasis on healthy lifestyles, there is an unprecedented proportion of the population who are grossly overweight and despicably out of shape. We eat as though there will be no food tomorrow.

Drinking has become a national epidemic. I speak from firsthand experience, although I have never tasted alcohol in my life. My father drank himself to death when he was thirty-three years old, leaving my mother with five little children to raise on her own. I was only four-and-a-half years old. His self-proclaimed license to drink deprived all of us of the privilege of having a father/guide in our lives. At age forty-one my oldest sister drank herself to death. Probably more accurately, it was a combination of drugs and alcohol that brought about her untimely death. What do I know about drinking? Must one experience personally the terrible life-threatening fight against addiction to know about something?

Like you, I grew up during the days when drug abuse went from using too much aspirin, through marijuana, and on to crack, heroine, LSD, and other permanently mind-altering drugs. What a waste to see people sell their integrity, morals, and their very lives to support an addictive habit. We will never be able to legislate drug control until the people decide to take control of their own lives and avoid using them. Then there will be no need for legislation. From your vantage point, you are in a unique position to help the young see that when you dance to the sound of the piper, the day will surely come when the piper must be paid. You cannot act with impunity when it comes to self-indulgence.

Another epidemic sweeping the country is what this generation has termed "the new morality." It is no more or less than the old "immorality" packaged under a new name. The early sixties produced the "free love" generation. Moral restraints were thrown to the wind. Fidelity in marriage was mocked as outdated. Love and sex were used as synonyms. Freedom at last from the restrictive, puritanical traditions of our fathers! Was it freedom? Now we are faced with the terrible waste of life to AIDS, STD (sexually transmitted diseases), divorce, and the like. It seems that our world has become so focused on sex that the only part of the person that is important is between the navel and the knees! How tragic.

That which we focus our attention on becomes important. We have outlawed the mention of God in the classroom and have enthroned the god of atheism and wonder why the family is breaking down and morals have hit an all-time low. It requires the wisdom of the aged to see that immorality (under whatever name it is masqueraded) is destructive to everyone it touches. Teenagers seem to have the most difficult time seeing why they should wait for sex until marriage and then be totally faithful within marriage. Our generation has lived long enough to see that "free love" is a misnomer. There is a terrible price associated with unlicensed sex outside marriage. Instead of bringing happiness, it brings sorrow, hatred, and mistrust. Instead of freedom it brings slavery. Instead of cementing relationships, immorality destroys all relationships.

Whether you learned these truths by being taught or by sad experience, you have probably lived long enough to be able to stand as a witness of the correctness and wisdom of what God revealed 3,500 years ago atop Mt. Sinai—thou shalt not commit adultery. Unfortunately, Moses couldn't stay around long enough to renew that command to each generation. Perhaps the Lord expects us to renew the command. Remember that Moses was over eighty years old when he received the commandment! Perhaps you who are eighty or older could be equally as effective in pointing out the pitfalls associated with unlicensed sex.

This chapter could be enlarged into an entire volume with little or no effort. Perhaps a summary principle in the form of several questions will suffice. If you had life to live all over again, what do you wish you had known at the beginning that you are starting to realize now? What changes would you make in what you did, how you spent your time and resources, how you disciplined your children, how you treated your spouse, and so on? If you will spend some time thinking through the answers to these questions and the many others that will present themselves to your mind, you will be equipped to fulfill the challenge of this chapter. Use the wisdom of the ages to bless the lives of those who desperately need your help. If you don't, there is a pretty good chance that they will not be around to read this book when they are your age.

If I had a choice between bringing the brightest minds in the entire world, who teach in the greatest universities and colleges of the world, together to compile a book of wise sayings, or to gather an equal number of senior citizens together for the same purpose, I would (without hesitation) summon the latter group. Collectively and individually you have so much to give, without which our quality of life will continue to deteriorate until we self-destruct. Will that happen? It depends on you. If you give your all, you will brighten our future. If you choose the easy route and pull your world in around you, we will not have to worry about a safe, moral world for our grandchildren to grow up in—there won't be one. Please, for the benefit of the world, use your wisdom to bless all mankind.

Chapter 6

"IN MINE OWN DUE TIME"

As we approach the conclusion of our lives, it may be that we would like to increase the tempo so we can accomplish all we want to do or make up for that which we didn't do. Sometimes our physical condition precludes us from being able to "run, and not be weary; and . . . walk, and not faint" (Isaiah 40:31). So much to do and so very little time and strength to do it in. How are we to react?

Remember all of those projects that you thought you "had" to do? If you didn't get them done, what happened? The sun still came up the next morning; the world did not fall to pieces; and miraculously human life did not cease to exist. Very often those things that we see as absolutely essential are little more than something that would be nice.

For so many aging parents and grandparents, we look with anxious gazes at the approach of death and wonder whether we will have time to help our children find their way in life, or time to help recover a grandchild from wayward paths. Just as with all the other projects we started but didn't quite get finished, so will it be in the lives of our family. In my doctoral program, the professors used two terms rather freely: formative and summative. "Formative" means whatever quality or characteristic is being considered, it is still in the process of being formed, molded, or improved upon. "Summative" means that the formative stage is over and the result is not subject to any additional change.

Using those definitions, life is formative! Life is dynamic and always subject to change. I have long since refrained from "writing off" the people I work with. Just when I am absolutely certain that a certain person will never change, I get a letter from them thanking me for not giving up on them and telling me about what they are doing. It is good I read my mail sitting at my desk because more often than not, I'd fall down from shock. Addicts do kick the habits. Irresponsible youth do become responsible adults. Insensitive children do become sensitive, loving, and (sometimes) almost doting over their aging parents.

If the world hasn't given up on me yet and I am still able and allowed to make whatever mid-course corrections I deem necessary and desirable, why should I do less for any fellow member of the human race? I am not advocating that we indulge the blatant law breaker. If a person takes another person's life, it is right that he or she should forfeit (perhaps for the rest of their lives) the freedom to mingle among their fellow men. Laws need to be established and enforced for the good and safety of society. However, when the mistakes we make fall more into the category of blunders or follies, I am totally committed to more patience and forgiveness.

Over the years you have probably noticed that there seems to be an unseen clock that controls our lives more than we do. Life, in fact, seems to be built in the reverse from what we think it should be. Young married couples with families may have more time and not enough money to do all they would like to do. Those who are older often have the money, but there isn't enough time to do everything they want to do. When we were young, we may have had the energy and strength to climb mountains and do the impossible. When we get older, we often have the wisdom to know what is impossible coupled with little strength and energy to do what is necessary. When we were young we had the capability to bear children but not the wisdom to rear them without making some serious errors. Now in old age, we have the wisdom to raise children and (thankfully) not the capability to bear children.

Perhaps in our present condition of knowing more than we understand, we would make the mistake (if we had the ability) of restructuring the clock of mortality. Thankfully, we don't have that option. We grow older just one day at a time. We can't go back and relive or undo what we experienced earlier. But we have greater say over what we will do in the future. If we view life as summative because we cannot go back and change the past, then we fail to appreciate the fact that we are not the same person today that we were fifty years ago. If we look at the totality of life as being formative, then we will realize that there may be opportunities ahead of us for continued growth. Given an eternity, how many more changes could be made?

So, it should be with regard to our children and grandchildren. We ought to do all we can to help them establish a life that will result in happiness and peace. If they choose to exercise their agency and go in a different direction, we should never withdraw our love for them, even if we detest their behavior. Perhaps they may even change their perspective as they surround your open grave.

It is tempting to dictate to the Master clock setter when certain things should take place. Often when they do not happen, we are tempted to either deny His existence or become disillusioned with the way our life is going. You have lived long enough to see that some of the things you may have viewed as tragedies in your early life actually turned out to be your greatest blessings and benefactors.

In the last chapter I mentioned my father dying when I was very young. For many years I looked upon his passing as a sign of Divine displeasure. About the time I was leaving my teenage years, I received a "revelation"—a real insight. I had noticed that while other boys and girls had fathers to guide them, they often took them for granted. Many times they would disregard their counsel and get punished for their misbehavior. Often, as a young man, I wished I had a father to correct me. But because I didn't, I became a people watcher. Now instead of being limited to one father, I had thousands! I looked for and analyzed the husband/wife relationship in every home I entered. I did it because I didn't know how a real husband and wife interacted. It dawned on me that for my future marriage, the death of my father may have blessed me.

Satisfied at that revelation, I continued living my life. I became aware that people were asking for my advice on how to discipline and raise their children. How was I to know? I wasn't even married. But intuitively I seemed to know the answer. Again, it dawned on me that I had watched a thousand fathers and mothers interact with their children. I had watched because I knew someday I would be a father, and I didn't have a role model to follow because my father had died. Almost unconsciously I had made a list of positive ways of dealing with children and a list of those ways that did not work as well. Wow! A second revelation. Because of my father's death, I was better equipped to deal with some of the frustrations associated with rearing children.

Life goes on as life does. One day a fellow faculty member brought a grieving child to my classroom. He said, "I'll teach your class while you talk to Bob. His father was just killed in a car accident." I put my arm around Bob's shoulder and escorted him into my office. I expressed my sympathy and ended by saying, "I know how you feel."

With defiant bitterness in his eyes he hissed back, "How could you possibly know how I feel?"

When I told him my dad had died when I was young, his whole demeanor changed. During the next fifteen minutes we talked openly and freely about life after death, how he could go on with his life, some of the pitfalls to avoid, and how to help the rest of his family adjust. At the conclusion of our interview, we left my office. We were both laughing over some play on words one of us had made. The teacher who had brought Bob to me was dumbfounded. "How did you do that?" he queried. Revelation number three. I knew how to handle the situation because I had experienced the same thing myself.

Over the years the revelations have just kept coming. My father's death enabled me to empathize and counsel with power. Yes, I missed out on a lot of things because my father wasn't in the home, but I was compensated by the lessons I learned that I likely would not have otherwise learned. When one door closes a dozen other doors open that were not available to you before.

Often, we make the terrible mistake of judging God based upon our limited vision and experience here in life. When a child dies, when a spouse or loved one is maimed or killed in an accident, or when an unfortunate turn of events renders us in difficult straits, we are prone to blame God. Perhaps an illustration will help me make my next point.

Do you remember the home you grew up in? My mother's home is over one hundred years old. It had the old skeleton key locks on the doors. After my mother was widowed, she used to invite her friends to come visit for a coffee party. Not wanting to be disturbed by little children, she would give us a choice: either we could go outside and play or play quietly in the next room. One would think that little kids would choose to play outside. Generally, we chose to play in the adjacent room to where Mom and her friends were meeting. We loved the smell of the coffee rolls, and knew we would get whatever was left over. To ensure that they wouldn't be interrupted, Mom would lock the door and slip the skeleton key in the pocket of her apron. We in turn would rotate, taking turns looking through the keyhole to see what they were doing in the other room. My mother would position herself in front of the door (she was probably afraid we would bolt through the door and interrupt her party). One time she would be looking to her right laughing at something she could see going on in the room, but we couldn't see because of the restrictive field of view of the keyhole. The next time we would look through the keyhole, she would be looking very seriously to the left, concentrating on something that one of her friends was saying, but we could neither see nor hear. Our limited view can be compared to the restricted view we have of the whole plan for our lives.

If we look at God as being in the room called eternity, able to see from before we were born until long after we die, and if we look at ourselves being in the adjacent room called mortality, only able to look into eternity through a small keyhole, we see how ridiculous it is to dictate to God how to control what He can see from within the room. He has been watching mankind for thousands of years and says that He knows the end from the beginning. Since He really is our Father, we must assume that He would not cause or allow anything to happen to us that would be eternally detrimental to us.

Let's consider one more example. Say you were looking through the keyhole and saw six men dressed in long robes, each wearing a mask. They were surrounding a table with a naked woman strapped to the table and the lead man had a razor-sharp knife in his hand. What would you surmise was happening? Could it be a satanic ritualistic sacrifice? Perhaps. If you could see one-half hour before and see that the naked woman was nine months pregnant and diagnosed as not being able to give birth to the child naturally, and that an emergency C-section was necessary in order to save her life and the life of the baby, and that the six men were all highly trained doctors skilled in their area of expertise, would it make a difference in the way you viewed the scene? If you could see into the recovery room an hour and a half later and see the proud new father holding his son for the now-recovering wife and mother to see, and you could see their unbounded happiness and their thankfulness to the team of doctors for performing this miracle, would it further alter your original judgment?

Can we accept that many things that will happen to us during this life are not clearly understandable from our present knowledge and experience base? I have watched people mourn at the death of a loved one and in turn become angry at God for taking them. Are we suggesting that living in this world is preferable to living in the presence of God? Are we audacious enough to believe that we know better than God what is good for our loved one?

Perhaps it takes the aging process of life to help us realize that living here in mortality is not the most desirable condition. As our bodies begin to fall to pieces a little at a time, as we begin to lose our hearing, sight, taste, and control over bodily functions, it becomes more apparent that earth life is meant to be temporary. When we see that clearly, we begin to look for ways of maximizing our time on earth, but (even given the opportunity) we decide that death is not as foreboding as we thought when we were young.

Of course, that is where this chapter is heading. The vision you have about life and death changes as you age. How can young people learn that death isn't always an irreversible tragedy? It will generally come through association with and instructions by those who have lived long enough to see more as God sees.

Why do people have to get old and sick? Why is there so much suffering associated with earth life? Why do bad things happen to good people? Is tragedy and suffering a sign of Divine displeasure? Many are the questions, and precious few are the definitive answers. But without a vision of earth life that has more direction and purpose than just mere existence, there are no concrete answers. When we view life as formative, we begin to see that the older we get, the more refined and polished we become. That refining is often painful and inconvenient. Just when we have the freedom and resources to do what we want to do, our health begins to fail. It hardly seems fair. Life is not fair if we look at birth as the beginning and death as the end. But if this life is just a very small segment of something that started years before, and is destined to continue on forever after, then we may rest assured that eventually fairness and equity will be achieved.

There is a calming effect in the mind of man when he begins to accept the things he cannot change and make the best of them. Of course, we should change everything we can that will make our life more enjoyable and easier. But the ability to discriminate between those things we can change and those things we can't adds greatly to our being able to accept graciously what happens to us.

So how do we help those who are coming after us? Sometimes it requires those with more vision to broaden the perspective of those who are following. If mothers did not explain to their daughters the pain of childbirth nor the joy that follows, many would likely face the experience with paralyzing fear. If fathers and mothers do not impress upon their children the difficulty of graduating from college, the children may likely opt for the more immediate but less satisfying job at a fast food restaurant. Part of the deferred gratification we willingly endure comes from the vision of greater rewards in the future. That vision is usually painted by those who have lived long enough to see further down the road than the youth.

In the midst of confusion associated with a hurricane, it is imperative to have someone who is calm and reassuring. Usually that person has weathered the storms before. Life is exactly like that. When the storm clouds gather around us in such a foreboding way, it is easy for young people to become anxiety ridden. To have someone there who is calm and reassuring can make all the difference in the world. When the nearly constant storms of life succeed in tipping over the furniture in our homes, it is comforting to have someone there who can reassure us that the storms will pass and times of peace and quiet will return. When asked by anxious young voices when that time will come, the older, more seasoned travelers of life will reassuring say, "In mine own due time. When the Lord is ready everything will happen as it is supposed to"

Whether we go through the storms of life or not is not left to our discretion. How we weather them is of supreme importance. Be the beacon light in the watchtower that sends out the stabilizing, reassuring beams of light when vulnerable sailors are in peril of shipwrecking on the hidden shoals of life. You were raised up for this very purpose. Don't disappoint the Master Seaman in His quest to bring all His children home safely through the storms.

Chapter 7

LIVE UNTIL YOU DIE

Doesn't everyone "live until you die?" Not really. Many years ago I saw a cartoon drawing of a tombstone. The caption read: "Died at twenty; buried at eighty!" For some reason the thought really stuck with me, although I have only used it once in teaching. While I was teaching at a high school, a senior girl came up after the last day of class and said, "That is the last book I will ever open in my life!" I said to her, "Then they could appropriately put on your grave marker 'died at eighteen and buried at eighty.'" She couldn't figure out what I was saying. So, I explained that when you stop growing and progressing you die even if your heart is still beating and you continue to exist for many more years.

The title of this chapter and also of this book came from a comment I made to my paraplegic uncle who I have referred to several times already. The last couple of years were not easy. His diminished lung capacity made it a chore to fight for every breath. The only time I ever heard him discouraged was when he had experienced a particularly difficult breathing session. I happened to drop in for a visit, and he commented that he was about ready to throw in the towel. In a spontaneous, yet rather self-righteous response I said, "Clyde, you can't quit now! Too many people are looking to you for strength to go on. You must 'live until you die.'" This homespun philosopher didn't respond immediately. He studied the floor for a couple of minutes and then said, "Randy, that's probably the most profound thing I've ever heard out of your mouth." The more I have thought about it, the more I can see why he thought it was profound.

From the first moment of birth, we have been learning, growing, progressing, accumulating information, cataloging experiences, making sense out of seemingly senseless situations, and increasing in wisdom. Life has not been easy, no matter who you are. It seems that life was designed to be a test of what we are made of. Probably each one of us have been tempted to quit many times. Sometimes, for reasons not fully understood by us, we have continued trying. There may have been seasons of discouragement and maybe even some depression. There have been times when you were sure that you couldn't take any more, and yet you did take it and you did keep going. There may have even been times when you wished (afterwards) that you had quit, but those times "came to pass." Thankfully they did not "come to stay." Even though there have been seasons of storm and cold, there have been many seasons of sunshine and happiness. Perhaps it will require an eternal review from the next world before we will fully understand why we have been subjected to everything we have.

What does it mean to "live until you die"? No matter how many of your faculties are deteriorating, or how many of your physical assets are becoming liabilities, you still have something left. If you didn't, you would not be able to read this book. Look back on your life at the things you loved to do in days gone by. Are you absolutely sure you cannot do them again, or at least a modified version of them?

Too often we place ceilings on ourselves that are artificially low. While it may be a statement of fact that you cannot run and jump like you did when you were young, it may not be true that you must be confined to a wheelchair. Recent research has shown that seniors as old as ninety years old have benefited greatly from a regular exercise program. Some who have been bedridden for years have not only broken the invisible shackles that kept them in bed, but have also eventually evolved into active, outgoing walkers and joggers. Could a miracle be in your future? There will always be voices, both verbal and silent, who will tell you that you can't do it. Most of the great accomplishments in life are successfully completed over the negative voices of the pessimists. What do you have to lose? If you give it your very best shot and still cannot get out of bed or leave the wheelchair, so what? You are already in bed or in a wheelchair.

A friend of mind died a while back. She was my piano teacher when I was a young boy. I wasn't such a good student, but it wasn't because she wasn't a superb teacher. She was in her nineties when she died. She had a stroke that left her partially paralyzed. As she lay on the couch crying over her inability to freely move as she had done for so many years, she saw the love of her life—her piano. According to her story, she went on a serious pity party for a few days, bemoaning the fact she would never play again. Then the old spunk came back. She had a goal. Without telling anyone about her resolve, she decided she would play again before she died.

It was not an easy task, and she confided that many times she wanted to give up. She told me this after she had beautifully played for me one of my favorite pieces. I have almost concluded that the only ceiling we have on what we can accomplish are artificially set by ourselves. Even if her one hand had never responded, she was so accomplished that the music she created with the other would have been the envy of all her friends.

Another senior friend dug out his oil paints, brushes, and canvas and started painting again after years of thinking he was too old to do good work. Some of his finest and most sensitive paintings were done long after retirement. It may require some adjustments from your original method of doing things. Perhaps you will have to work from a picture or a slide rather than being able to travel to the actual location.

A senior "used-to-be" rodeo friend has long passed the time when he could rope and ride. For years he attended every rodeo in this state and adjacent states. When his health precluded him from going, he started braiding leather whips, horse halters, and other paraphernalia that are in high demand by rodeo people. Now the rodeo crowd comes to him rather than him going to them. He is still very much a part of a scene that he has lived and loved all his life. Where there is a will, there is a way. It may require some serious creative thinking to find a way of staying involved when the body says "no," but find it you will.

When I was younger, I had an operation on my shoulder to fix a torn ligament. The nature of the operation required that the arm be immobilized for a month. At the end of the month, I anxiously looked forward to resuming work and activity. To my disappointment, the muscles in my arm had atrophied from lack of use. It took months of painful exercise before my arm was as strong as the other one. Perhaps that is the way it is with our minds. When we fail to use them, they may begin to atrophy. Just as with my inactive arm, your mind can be strengthened by strenuous use. It may be that you forget what you are reading before you even finish the page. Don't be discouraged or frustrated. Keep trying. Take some notes; ask yourself questions about what you are reading; discuss what you're reading with others. Within a very short time, you will find your mind actually is retaining more than it was before—even if it is far from an intellectual trap. As time goes on, your memory will continue to improve. I have another friend in his late eighties who memorizes poetry. Everyone is amazed at his ability to remember. He just keeps at it. What was so difficult (and he thought impossible) and challenging at first, he now laughs at as "kid's stuff."

I am writing this book using a computer. At first computers scared me to death. I was afraid I would touch a key and destroy everything I had worked so hard to create. Now I look back and laugh at my silliness. Although I have messed some documents up sufficiently that it required a person with greater skills than I have (usually one of our children) to come straighten me out, I have yet to blow up a computer or even to crash the hard drive. What a blessing the computer has been. I'm still a little shy around the internet, but my next project will be to get someone to teach me how to find my way around so I can freely communicate with people of similar interests around the world. Next, I will move on to Facebook, Twitter, blogging, instant messaging, and so on. Would this be an area you would like to get involved in if you could set aside your fears?

We live in a world where knowledge is exploding at such a rate that even the bravest souls question whether they can keep up. If you try and fail, so what? You probably don't use the internet now. What will happen if you never learn to use it? You have nothing to lose and everything to gain.

When I graduated with my doctorate degree a number of years ago, everyone in the 15,000-seat auditorium stood and gave a standing ovation. Not to me or the other successful doctoral candidates but to an eighty-two-year-old great-grandmother who had decided at age seventy-five that one of her lifelong goals was to graduate from a major university. I found myself among the standing, applauding thousands as they mentioned her by name and asked her to stand. She stole the entire show—and she deserved it. Is there an educational goal you have secretly had for all these years that you would like to accomplish before the end?

I happened to make acquaintance with this eighty-two-year-old graduate some time later. I asked her if she wasn't afraid that she might not be able to compete with the younger people. She said she was "scared spitless" but decided that she would never know unless she gave it a try. She said that there were times when she wondered if she was out of her mind. It took her seven years to complete a four-year degree, but the look on her face was evidence enough that the sacrifice had been well worth the effort. I asked her if she was going to use her degree to start a new career. Although I was only joking, she said she had thought about it but hadn't made up her mind if that was the direction she wanted to go at this point in her life. What a woman! Her attitude is the key to her success. She has an unconquerable spirit that inspires everyone in her presence. There is no question in my mind that she will be living and growing and doing until the day she dies.

One of my senior friends who passed away recently had become known in the latter years of his life as a master at crocheting doilies and knitting afghans. I saw some of his work. This is a man who was the "work outside, leave the inside stuff to the women" type of guy. When he was diagnosed with cancer and other physical factors that precluded his working outside, he decided that rather than vegetate he would learn to crochet. He said at first he wasn't very good but he kept practicing. Finally someone complimented him on his work and from then on nothing could stop him. Before he died, everyone who saw his work stood back in shocked amazement at his creations. Are there talents you may never have considered that could hold some appeal for you? Although this good man could have sold his work for a lot of money, he was not interested in increasing his wealth. He did this work out of love. He freely gave, which seemed to only magnify his satisfaction. Some of you may want to turn your new hobby into a money-making venture. There certainly isn't anything wrong with being paid for that which you love to do.

I was flying to California a while back to give a lecture. The plane was delayed slightly for an elderly couple in wheelchairs. They were helped into seats adjacent to mine. During the flight we struck up a conversation. I asked them if they flew much. To my surprise they said that they did. He had been a successful physician who retired many years ago. Money was no hindrance to them. Their children (five of them) lived in different parts of the country. On a regular basis this sweet couple flew to visit their children, but as they embarrassingly confided in me, more to see and get acquainted with their grandchildren. They assured me that they tried not to be a burden or impose on their children. They tried to leave while their children (and especially the grandchildren) still tried to talk them into staying longer. During each visit, they tried to share some lesson they had learned in life that they thought would be beneficial to their children and grandchildren. They said they make the rounds about three or four times a year, and the children all try to visit them at least once a year for a family reunion. I got the distinct impression from talking with them that they are forging chains of love, family, and traditions that will continue long after they move on to the next life.

We took my mother along with our family to *Phantom of the Opera*. She really enjoyed it and said it was the first opera she had ever attended. I happened to be seated next to a woman who was at least in her mid-eighties. She was alone, but not really. She didn't have anyone sitting by her except me, but before, during the intermission, and after the production she had people coming to talk with her. She obviously (I inferred from the comments I overheard) was a frequent visitor to the opera. Her lack of a partner, friend, or spouse to attend with her did not deter her in the least. She was as excited discussing the production with her friends, both old and young, as if she had been part of the production. Special provisions were made in the opera hall for wheelchairs. What a wonderful way of enjoying the talents of other people who are still young enough to be the participants rather than just the observers.

I need to stay away from one of my mom's friends. Don't take me wrong; she is a delightful person. Also well into her eighties, she never misses a college football or basketball game. She knows all the players by their first names. She can quote the statistics of each of the games, who won, who made the points, what their national (or league) standing is, and so on *ad infinitum*. The reasons I need to avoid her are twofold: 1) she talks longer than I have time for, and 2) she knows so much more than I do about sports that it makes me look really stupid. She is a great person. The players don't seem to mind high-fiving her after the games.

Church work, civic work, volunteer work, and much more are crying for willing participants. If you are willing to get outside yourself, there is no end to the projects you will find yourself involved in. Ask your priest or minister if there are jobs around the church house that need attention. I drove past a beautiful church in California on a recent trip and saw a group of senior women planting flowers around the church. One woman so impressed me that I drove past the church several times to watch her. She was evidently unable to walk. Her wheelchair was positioned about fifty feet from where she was working. It was pretty obvious from the soiled condition of her slacks that she had to crawl from place to place. The other women would do their plantings and then stand up and move to the next spot. This good woman scooted on her side and knees from place to place. No one seemed overly concerned nor was the woman self-conscious. The beauty of the finished project was reward enough to justify the dirty slacks and mud under the fingernails.

In the last chapter I wrote about the wisdom of the aged. What a tragedy if you went to your grave with your life's history locked inside your mind. Have you ever considered writing a book? Perhaps you say, "That's all we need is one more book!" True, if your book is intended just to sell copies. If that were the case, you could write about crime, violence, and sex. The entire market is saturated with books with those orientations. Who is more qualified to write about the great lessons of life than you? Perhaps publishing a book is not a goal. At least take the time and expend the energy to write down your personal history for your children and grandchildren. You may think that nothing exciting has ever happened to you. Let your posterity decide that! What seems common and mundane to you may be of vital interest to those who follow you. The day to day pioneer life of my great-grandmother is so foreign to my children that they would sit for hours listening to her story as we read it to them.

Maybe your children or grandchildren are not in the mental state right now to learn the lessons you have to teach. You could become offended and not share the lessons, or you could write them down and leave them for a time when they are more eager to learn from you. Written records can perpetuate your personality, your wit, your humor, your thinking, and your testimony about life for as long as the record is available. Although the scriptures are inspired declarations of prophets, they are also their journals and diaries of what transpired during their lifetimes.

There is another benefit of writing your life's history—you will be forced to reconstruct what has happened to you. It was not until I started writing my history that I became aware of the many areas that were positively influenced by the death of my father, as I mentioned in an earlier chapter. It would have been too bad if I had lived my entire life with feelings of bitterness against my father for dying (something he had only partial control over) before I matured. It will be in the writing of your history that it dawns on you why certain things happened, or what lessons you actually learned, or counsel you want to give your family to help them avoid some of the rough spots of life.

Life is too short to die at twenty and wait until eighty or ninety to be buried. There is so much to do, so many lives to influence, so many neat experiences to have, so many mountains (physical, social, mental, and spiritual) to climb that we can't afford to waste another minute. No matter where you are in the "melt-down" stage of life, there is still time to continue living. When all of your faculties have shut down, you will be unaware that there is life to live, so it won't matter anyway. Until then, take control and "live until you die."

Chapter 8

NOT FAST BUT STEADY

Judging from the title of this chapter, you may assume you know right where I am going. While the first part of the chapter will deal with the slowing-down process and how to deal with it, the second part of the chapter will broaden the concept into an area that may require time and thought to put into perspective and practice.

As the body begins to refuse to move at the breakneck speeds of youth, there are changes that need to be made. These changes are not all bad; in fact, most are very desirable. While I was in college, the Vietnam War was still being fought. Although we were not unwilling to join the armed services, we wanted to complete our schooling before enlisting. By enrolling in ROTC (Reserve Officer's Training Corps) we could not only defer our entry date but also better our position to that of an officer when we enlisted.

Part of our training took place at a winter camp during the break between college semesters. As younger men, we were assigned to capture a hill where the "enemy" was holed up. We were given maps, radios, binoculars, and a set of detailed instructions on how to proceed. It was sort of fun—like a game. We met before leaving for our objective to map out our strategy. However, we felt the verbal instructions had been good enough; we didn't need to read all the small print on the instruction page. After separating into groups, devising hand signals (we had correctly surmised that the "enemy" would have radios on the same frequency as our own so they would be able to listen in on our conversations), and establishing sequences of moves, we set out.

We moved stealthily toward the objective, taking every precaution not to be detected. Minutes evolved into hours as we painstakingly surrounded the hill and started our ascent. We were bursting with pride and confidence as we continued our assault and met no resistance. The senior students (who were the enemies), must be asleep, we thought. Perhaps we had taken them entirely off guard.

When we arrived at the top of the hill, to our amazement and total frustration, we had "captured" the wrong hill! Only a few hundred yards away we saw the "enemy" pointing and laughing at us. Embarrassed at our mistake, we pulled out the instruction sheet. Item number one read, "Make sure of your location. Do not capture the wrong objective!" What a blow to the ego. Perhaps we will never live down that mistake.

Although our mistake was embarrassing, it did little or nothing to detour us from our chosen course in life. However, surrounding the wrong mountains in real life can cost us precious time that cannot be recovered. When the body begins to wear out, we realize that we can't "capture" every mountain. We have to make some difficult choices based on our long-range goals. As a young child, I wanted to be a policeman and a fireman and a scientist and an astronaut and a sea captain. I also wanted to be Tarzan, Lord of the Jungle, and a host of other movie characters. But even as a child I realized that I couldn't be everything.

At this point in our lives, it is even more imperative that we stop and take multiple "mid-course corrections." Some trails are shorter but more difficult to climb. Wise is the person who calculates the cost before beginning the climb. It may take longer to reach your destination by choosing the longer, more gradual path. But if you keep at it, you are more likely to make it than by taking the shorter, more direct, but more difficult path. The old fable of the tortoise and the hare comes to mind. Sometimes the race is not won by the swift but by the steady.

As I look back on my life, there are so many things I could have done faster and more efficiently if I had only taken a little more time to make sure I was aiming at the right target. We use two words (incorrectly but sometimes interchangeably) that describe the phenomenon: precision and accuracy. A person can be exactingly precise and miss the entire target because they did not accurately aim at the right target. If you get exactly what you aim for in life, will you be disappointed in what you hit?

You may remember the first manned moon flight. As the world was permitted to listen to the transmissions between the spaceship and the control center, I was surprised at how frequently they would fire the rocket's engines for just a few seconds to make mid-course corrections. If they had not given attention to those small details, the spacecraft would have entirely missed the objective (the moon) and flown endlessly into space.

At times it is difficult to accurately define what we want from life. Taking sufficient time to look beyond the present to the ultimate target is something most youth and many adults fail to do very well. I mentioned earlier that my father had a drinking problem. Had he looked beyond the moment and followed his unbridled indulgence to its logical conclusion, he would have seen that no good could result from his behavior. Instead he, and many like him, continued on as though tomorrow would never come. When it did come, it was too late to make the massive mid-course correction necessary to salvage the mission.

Whether one considers husband/wife relationships, family relationships, physical limitations, social interactions, intellectual goals, or spiritual directions, without frequent mid-course checks and corrections, how will we ever arrive at our desired destination? Think of the number of people you know who are one hundred years old and still alive. Although there may be a few, they are precious few. Whatever they had wanted to do before exiting this life either had to be done then or be forever undone.

In light of the chapter title, "Not Fast but Steady," maybe the emphasis should be put on the "steady" rather than on the pace or tempo of the journey. Since we cannot be everything to everybody, let's make sure that we are at least something to somebody! It might be that we are spread so thin that there isn't enough of us to make a significant difference in any area. Could a mid-course correction be in order? Among the many possibilities in deciding what corrections need to be made, perhaps more time could be spent reading the Bible or other great books to help focus the target to increase the changes of an accurate hit.

Although there are many more things we could say about being steady and accurate, it seems appropriate to move on to the next line of thinking. Earth life seems to be made up of choices and priorities. We are free to choose the course we want to pursue in life, but if we make that choice and do not deviate, we are not free to choose the consequences or destination. For example, my oldest sister was free to choose to take the "drug and alcohol" route. She was not free to ignore the associated consequences. She died at age forty-one.

When we were young it seemed like we could pick up one end of a stick (an action or thought) and because the other end of the stick didn't immediately follow, we erroneously concluded that it would never follow. But it does follow, as we have discovered during our more mature years. I would like to refer to a couple of examples that are explosive and controversial to make my point. You may agree or disagree, but take the time to look at the principle behind the example that I am trying to teach.

Over the years there has been an increasingly heated debate over the issue of abortion. On the one hand people maintain (rightfully) that a woman should have control over her own body—the pro-choice people. The other camp argues that it is not an option to destroy an innocent human being (also correct). These are the pro-life people. Although I am taking this explosive issue as an example, the underlying principles are much broader.

Sometimes we focus on the correct issue but the wrong timing. A woman should definitely have control over her own body, but the focus should be on her right to choose whether or not to engage in an activity that could result in the creation of another human life. Once that choice has been made, the consequences (other end of the stick) should not be optional. I am painfully aware of the issues the pro-choice people use concerning women who are victims of rape and incest. But, the truth be known, they represent such a small percentage of the total that it is ludicrous to base the entire argument on the few cases that could and should be decided on an individual basis. Before continuing the example and making my point, let me add another factor.

Recently an argument erupted between the "animal protection people" and the "make a wish for a dying child" people. The dying wish of a young man was to go bear hunting in Alaska. He came from a family of hunters, and this would be heaven to him. The people who opposed on the other side of the issue decried the wanton destruction of animal life merely to satisfy a selfish wish. It was finally decided by the "make a wish" people to fund the hunting trip for the terminally ill young man. Please don't get caught up in the examples; that seems to be what the entire world is doing!

If the young man finds the bear he is hunting, takes careful aim, and pulls the trigger on his loaded and properly functioning rifle, the bullet will discharge and the result will be irreversible. It would be nonsense to argue, after he pulled the trigger, that he had changed his mind and didn't want the bullet to hit the aimed-at target. Once the trigger is pulled, the freedom to choose whether the rifle fires or not is not the real issue nor is it a viable option.

So it is with the abortion issue. Once the gun is fired (intercourse has taken place), it is not logical to then say whether the consequences should happen. Although many times conception does not occur, many times it does. If the bear is in the line of sight of the bullet, it will get hit. Sometimes the hunter is not too accurate and the bear escapes. If the hunter is accurate, the result is the destruction of a bear's life. If allowed to run its natural course, the result of human reproduction is a child. An abortion ends that process.

As I listen to the compelling arguments on both sides of the abortion issue, if I do not have a grasp of the whole picture, I can easily become confused about what to do. If I listen to both sides of the hunting/animal rights issue, it is equally as easy to become confused if you take those arguments in a vacuum. Now my point. Whatever position you take on the abortion issue or the animal rights issue or a million other issues like those, if you do not go slowly enough to weigh all the factors as they interrelate to each other, you may easily surround the wrong mountain. Youth (and many adults) get on a hobby horse and ride it to death. Turtles in California and Utah take precedence over homes for people. Owls in Oregon take priority over jobs for thousands of families. The list goes endlessly on. When we fail to take time to look at problems from every point of view, it is easy to become so adamant for our own point of view that we refuse to consider anyone else's opinion. I am not sure we will ever find a solution to the abortion problem, the animal right's issues, and the environmental concerns until we disengage long enough to allow others the same latitude and consideration we expect for ourselves.

Hopefully, the examples I used have not distracted you from the principles. As we mature, we learn that most problems, like the ones mentioned above, will not just go away. To solve them by killing each other hardly seems like a mature response. No matter how opposed I may be to abortion, killing innocent people at an abortion clinic has a strong stench of hypocrisy. When we kill protesters at a "save the owl" demonstration, we are missing the issue.

As long as we live in a human society (which will probably be until we die), we are going to need to learn to listen to each other, really communicate, negotiate, and compromise. The world seems to be in a divisive mode. A pile of individual bricks dumped on your lot has the same weight and the same volume as when they are beautifully laid by a master craftsman into a home for you and your family. In the pile, the bricks act as individuals and contribute very little to the whole. In the house, the individual bricks are vital to the stability and beauty of the structure. In society, individuals acting alone contribute little or nothing to the stability and beauty of the whole. When we work together we are essential to one another's well-being and continued safety.

Often that fact is not understood by the loud, blatant voices demanding change for the sake of change. They may be so naive as to believe that all change is good, or that it is a given to change from a bad situation to a better one. In reality, things could be much worse if the wrong changes are endorsed. It seems to require the wisdom and maturity of age to slow down the negotiation so tempers do not flare out of control with devastating results.

I was in a convenience store paying for my gas when a young man came in to buy a drink. In a childish act of frustration, he doubled up his fist and hit the ice machine because the ice did not immediately dispense when he pushed the button. The manager of the store yelled at him to stop abusing the machinery. Then, rather than merely walking to the machine and helping the young man, the manager threatened to knock his head like he had knocked the machine if he did it again. Not to be embarrassed in front of the other patrons in the store, the young man challenged the manager to step outside and see who was going to thump the other's head. The verbal duel degenerated from there. One ounce of maturity on the part of the manager could have defused the entire situation. Yes, the boy was wrong in hitting the machine. The manager was also wrong in provoking a confrontation. Both of them lost in the end no matter what the final outcome was.

Perhaps progress can be made when the pro-life and pro-choice people maturely agree to sit down and talk things through. When we try to identify the common beliefs before trying to resolve the differences, strange things happen. There are only a very few issues that the two sides differ on. When each side sees the others as totally depraved, godless people, fanatics without the ability to reason, is it any wonder they are reluctant to sit and talk through the issues? Owls and timber cutter jobs are not the issue. Can a solution be reached where both can accomplish their objective?

Until we start to identify problems and then seek to find acceptable solutions, I am afraid we will only see more senseless destruction of human life. Although both sides on every issue have demands, there is enough time to find a reasonable solution. The eminent destruction prophesied by both sides of every issue seldom materialize. There are doomsday prophets who forecast the end of society over every single issue.

In the event that you are willing to be the rational mind in a mindless argument, it might be helpful to use a method used in philosophy. It is called "prior question." Whenever a person or group asks a question, the moderator of the argument asks himself, "Is there a prior question?" That means, is there something else the person or group needs to understand before they can truthfully understand the answer to their question? For example, a young couple may ask, "How do we get out of debt?" A prior question might well be, "Do you understand how to budget?" or maybe even a prior question like, "Do you understand the principle of buying on credit versus deferred payments?" As a teacher, I am asking "prior question" inquiries of myself constantly. Usually, if I make a big mistake in assuming that the students understand some foundational knowledge and they really don't, little learning takes place. It is difficult to erect the walls, put the roof on, and finish the house if there isn't a foundation under it!

As you take a deep breath and stand back to study the issues, consider one vital prior question: Is there a right and a wrong to this issue? No matter what we may believe, the ultimate rights and wrongs of life come from the fact that we either accept or reject God as the revealer of all truth. Adultery is wrong because God revealed that it is wrong. We may want to argue with Him, but if we accept Him as the lawgiver, then what He says is right is right and what He says wrong is wrong!

If you choose to deny the existence of God, you complicate the issue of right and wrong because then the vote of the ever-shifting majority determines what is right and wrong. During the last half century, ample evidence exists showing that according to the whims of fickle man, what is right today is wrong tomorrow and is right again the next day. As a senior member of the human race, it may well fall on your shoulders to defy modern tradition and actually mention the role that God plays in our decision-making processes. If you were in an educational setting, you would be mandated against by law. In society and in private life, you may have a chance to bring some sanity back into the way we make decisions. If we have no foundation upon which to build our decisions, we shouldn't be too surprised if the structure is unsafe from the very beginning. If we build on two separate and conflicting foundations (atheism and theism), the structure will also likely have little or no stability. We must get back to a basic foundation, and that can only be done by refusing to take our pistols to the negotiating table.

Standing on the sidelines and screaming at each other is not likely to produce solid, well-thought-out results. It may very well fall to those of us who cannot run away from the battle to bring sound reasoning into the discussions. Your ability to take criticism without blowing up, or to be misrepresented without blowing the accuser away, may be the determining factor in saving our society. Be wise enough not to succumb to the temptation to "count yourself out" just because the snows of winter are permanently affixed to your hair. I have found that the best solutions to insolvable problems often come after consulting with aged and experienced people. Yes, the bubbly effervescence of youth is fun, but the slow, sure pace of the elderly is what excites confidence. Be the one in your group who dares to make a calm, rational statement about electric, volatile issues.

Chapter 9

LIFE AFTER RETIREMENT

All of our adult lives we often looked forward to a time when we could retire from work and take life at a more sane and leisurely pace. Some are fortunate enough, or wise enough investors, to be able to retire while they are still relatively young and in good health. What you do with life after retirement may well flavor the entirety of your life.

While I worked my way through college, I was employed as an assistant to the county engineer. He was nearing retirement age sixty-five. At sixty-five he did retire from his governmental position. He worked for another twenty years in private business. I asked him why he continued to work since, financially, he was well set and certainly daily necessity did not require it of him. He responded by saying that too many of his friends had retired and within a year had been "planted in a three-foot by six-foot garden plot." He was afraid that if he ever stopped working he would die! His statement greatly intrigued me, so I started watching retired people to see how they reacted to their changed status.

Some people would sit on the porch day after day and never do anything—they were retired. Others became involved in the lives of their children and grandchildren, church, community, civic clubs, and so on until they were so busy they couldn't figure out how they ever had time to work. Those two scenarios were at the opposite ends of the continuum. Then there were people everywhere in between. Not everyone who sat on the porch died within the first year after retirement. Not everyone who became so busy they didn't have time to sit for a minute lived to a ripe old age. Some were happy and contented with retired life. Others were miserable and not very shy about letting people know they were miserable.

The determining factor seemed to be what people expected from life. If a person needed to be involved in some productive effort and was not, they soon passed away. If they thought they were too tired and they needed to rest and didn't get the rest, they passed away. If they wanted to be involved and were, they seemed to continue on as though life hadn't changed much. If they wanted the rest and got it, they seemed to do fine. It is up to you to determine how you want to fill your time. There is one thing for sure—everyone is given exactly the same number of hours in a day. The busy are not given more and the idle are not given less. It is not the amount of time but your expectations of how to use the hours that makes the difference on how you view your retirement years.

Is there a "right" and "wrong" way to spend your retirement years? The answer depends on your long-range goals. If your goal is just to make it to the end of life, satisfying your own personal needs, then how you spend your time doesn't make much difference. If you decide you want to make a difference in life, then your retirement years become a precious bonus. Using your accumulated resources (not just money and things but experiences, personality traits, and so on), you can decide where to make your presence felt. It may be with your family. You may decide that the church needs your time and talents. Civic clubs, community service, assisting in elementary schools, and volunteer service all represent areas where senior citizens are welcome and in desperate need.

Occasionally a retired couple will determine that they have some unique talents that could enrich a larger population than just their immediate area. Perhaps a mission would be in order. A particular man we have been close to for years had worked all of his professional life as an agricultural engineer at the local university. Upon retirement, he and his wife decided to help develop the irrigation systems in Honduras. Although they were employed by the government, their living conditions were much more primitive than their comfortable home. They struggled with the food, language, customs, and culture, but after two years of service they had enriched the lives of thousands of people. They came home to resume retired life and found that the grandchildren had lives of their own to live and they felt unneeded. They volunteered to return for another year to a people who needed them and loved them and really appreciated the sacrifices they were making for them. As we talk with them now, they count those years in Honduras as some of the most memorable of their lives.

Since returning from Honduras, they have served a mission in Australia and are currently in Syria helping hundreds of thousands of people live a more comfortable life. Such a life for a couple who retired but learned that enjoying life was more than porch sitting.

Other couples have volunteered with health services in developing countries. Although the media tends to sensationalize the one or two couples who suffer personal tragedy during their terms of service, there are thousands of people who take the wisdom of the aged and bless those whose lives would otherwise be much more difficult.

You may think you do not have a particular talent you could share. The things we take for granted are unheard of in developing countries. Several couples we know have volunteered to teach English in Mongolia to college students and professors. They have no formal education except that they are available and they speak English. Before you close the doors on the possibilities, contact the International Red Cross, the Job Corps, or an international embassy and find out if they need volunteers. Your church may have an organized mission to help the underdeveloped peoples of the world. It may amaze you how many doors are open that would provide the icing on the cake for a life well lived.

If you are willing, there will be so many individuals and agencies that will gobble up your time that you may need to learn to say "no." As you establish priorities in your lives, you will find it is relatively easy to keep first things first. If your family is first, then a call by the head of the local service club may have to wait until the family need has been satisfied. It is frustrating for those who do not understand priorities or have not firmly established priorities for themselves.

Over the years many people have given me advice (most of it is worth exactly what I paid for it—nothing). I have distilled a list of priorities that seem to work for me and for many others. In case you haven't consciously thought about prioritizing your life, you might consider this list. Adjust it as you see necessary or throw it away. It is only intended as a point to begin to take control of your own life.

The first priority for me is my wife. When everything is going well between us, I can handle the rest of life without too much trouble. When we are at odds, even the most minor problems cause me to stumble. If I put her in the first spot, I have an ally, a confidant, a helper to meet whatever challenge I face. When all of my other faculties give out, she will still be there. If I have neglected her or failed to develop a solid relationship, it will be to my own hurt later in life when she is all I have left to rely upon.

The second priority for me is my children and grandchildren. I seem to have a special stewardship or responsibility for them. Sometimes they are really demanding. Other times I hardly ever hear from them. I find that my first and second priorities are interrelated—more than just through marriage and blood! If I ignore my second priority, my first priority gets after my case. When I am diligently striving to meet the needs of my second priority, my number-one priority is a great source of support. As life progresses, I find that there isn't a constant demand by the family. There are seasons when they seem to be all-consuming. Other times I am only there for a backup in case their own time or resources are insufficient. I'm discovering that both cases are all right.

I find that if I ignore my own personal needs too long, I start to get grouchy, irritable, and hard to get along with. Therefore, my third priority is myself. I need to stay in good health and also have enough time to clear my mind and make sure I feel good about myself. Over the years I have counseled too many times with people who neglect themselves. The example I use with them is this: If you are the ship that is carrying your spouse, family, and others who rely on you, and your ship springs a leak, do you continue to tender to the needs of your passengers while your ship goes down? In that regard and to a limited measure, you must be your number-one priority. Usually, however, in meeting your spouse's personal needs and those of your family, you will discover that your needs are also being met. Therefore, I will leave my own personal needs as a third priority with the exception noted above.

Fourth is my obligation to the church. What can I do to help other people use the Bible and the gospel principles to cope with the challenges of life? I am technically not related to these people, but through the years our association has made us feel like family. Others who are not closely associated with a church may find that the people in your club or civic organization are the closest you can come to family. Perhaps the priority is to tend to the needs of those who are closest to being like family. That selfless service that you give freely to others seems to have a soul-satisfying effect on everyone who gives it. People seem most miserable who are totally "inward" focused. When I forget myself in the service of others, I seem to feel better about myself, have fewer problems, and am able to cope with the up's and down's of life better than when I give too much attention to myself.

My fifth priority is my work, profession, or vocation. After I have satisfied the priorities above, I have found it rewarding to ask, "Do I have any talents or skills that could be used to make life more pleasant for other people?" Without getting a swollen head, you must be able to admit where you are good, and where you have talents. Even though you may not be professionally trained, some of you are natural counselors. You will recognize this ability because every stray puppy you ever ran across has followed you home from the time you were little. You may have wondered why everyone confided their problems in you. Not everyone can counsel others. Some people radiate those qualities that enable other people to share their problems with them even after a very brief association. Some of you may be natural "fix-it" people. My wife is one of those. I am not very mechanically gifted, but she is. She takes apart the toaster oven and repairs it. I marvel at her abilities and wish I could learn her talent. She has never been trained—it just comes naturally.

Take a good look at your natural talents. They are usually things you like to do because you are good at them. Don't be afraid to use either your professionally trained talent or your natural talents to bless the lives of others. It helps to listen to what others say about you. Usually they are not saying things just to win your approval. People can be pretty honest when they compliment you about areas they perceive you are good at. As you continue to make yourself available (as time permits and as your desires are there), you may find yourself in higher demand than you can fulfill. You certainly would not be the first retired person to start another career after retirement just because you really love what you are doing.

A good friend of mine has always been interested in rock collecting. This "rock hound" retired as an engineer and opened his own lapidary shop. He loved cutting, polishing, and mounting semi-precious gems in jewelry. He was really good at it and made a lot of money doing what he loved to do. I think his only regret is that he didn't start in the business many years before.

The sixth priority for me is generated by a question I periodically ask myself, "What can I do to improve the world I live in?" Maybe the answer will be nothing, but—in the unlikely event that I have some spare time left over after the first five priorities are satisfied—maybe there is something I can do to help. My sole purpose in writing this book is to help others enjoy some of the success my wife and I are experiencing. No, we haven't arrived at perfection or even like unto it, but we are having a great time living our lives together with our families and friends.

Your list may be different than mine. You may have fewer or more items than I have. But I have discovered that if I take control of my life based upon predetermined priorities, I have fewer frustrations when I can't do everything for everybody.

Another factor I have observed in retired persons who seem to be happy is that they are willing to roll with the punches or shift their priorities with the passage of time. When we become so rigid that everything must happen as we dictate, we are setting ourselves up for failure. If one thing in life is constant, it is the inconsistency of life. There will always be emergencies, exceptions, and circumstances that require deviation from the plans. If you can't adjust, you will spend your life frustrated.

One couple I know decided that they really wanted to improve their golf game after the husband retired. Everything went well for a couple of years until he had a mild stroke that made it impossible for them to continue playing golf. At first, they went into a mild depression. Then one day they snapped out of it. The change was so dramatic that I questioned what had happened. They informed me that they had just reordered their priorities and that golf was no longer at the top of the list. Their frustration seemed to result from their having a goal and not being able to attain it. Their solution—change the goal! How simple. How practical!

Contrast that with another man who retired to a life of golf. He purchased the clubs, the bag, the shoes, the gloves, the entire regalia. He just needed one minor operation on a shoulder to repair an old football injury from years back. The operation was successful, although the doctor told him he might suffer some temporary numbness due to nerve damage. When the recovery was complete the numbness was there but expected. As weeks turned into months and the numbness did not leave, he became concerned. The doctor informed him that in an isolated case or two the numbness was permanent. He was unable to grip the golf clubs. He went into a depression. No one could help him through it. His life was ruined. What was the use of living? Instead of reordering his priorities, he resigned himself to a life of misery. Within the year he suffered a massive stroke and subsequently died. What would have been the difference if he had accepted the change in game plan and gone on with life after reordering priorities? Maybe the outcome would have been the same, but the way his family and friends viewed him for that last year would have been considerably different. He exited life a bitter, cantankerous old man whom no one liked to be around. It was an old man's temper tantrum. If it had been a child, the parents would likely have paddled him good and sent him to his room. As an adult he just succeeded in making everyone miserable.

In traveling around the country, I have noticed that in certain areas there are incredible organizations for seniors. Other areas are not so tuned into the needs of the seniors. Wherever you live, if you have the time, the interest, and the vitality, you can create your own hubbub of activity. Life does not stop when the work-a-day world stops. Here is your opportunity to make a significant contribution to society in general. If we sit around and expect the government to do something for us and smooth the rough spots in our road of life, we will be frustrated and angry during the entirety of the golden years of our lives. If we determine to take inventory of our resources and make the best of our time and efforts, miracles will be an everyday occurrence.

It does not seem to be what happens to us that is of supreme importance. It is more how we cope with the daily challenges of life. Attitude indeed seems to determine altitude. Financial setbacks during the later years do not need to signal the dismal end. A good friend of my mother's got the bad news that her stocks had taken a dive and she would no longer be receiving the dividend. She went into a depression. With her retirement, social security, and other investments she was receiving over $2,000 a month. Her home was paid for, her expenses were minimal, but she thought she would probably starve to death. Now instead of banking $3,000 a month, she can only put $1500 away. Perspective is important. Wallowing in self-pity when we have so much going for us is counterproductive.

Make the most of life. Even life after retirement is a time to glory in what you did right, learn from what you did wrong, and continue to live and build those you touch. Whether we die having expended our time and energy in a productive cause or sat idly by in self-service, the day we depart this life will still come. When it does, we only take with us what we have experienced, not what we have accumulated.

Chapter 10

GRACIOUSLY ACCEPTING THE INEVITABLE

Some things in life we can change, and some things we cannot. Recognizing the difference and being willing to live within the scope of the limitations externally imposed upon us results in a level of peace and contentment not known to those who refuse to comply. I don't know if there is a given day when the body begins to deteriorate. There probably is, but it is difficult to recognize and admit. It may be different for each individual. But it will eventually happen.

Remember the first time you realized that you were having to hold the newspaper farther away so the words would be in focus? "I'm too young for glasses!" is a phrase that I often used. For a number of years I refused to admit that my vision was blurry. It wasn't until I failed the eye exam for renewing my driver's license that I was confronted with the obvious. Although the optometrist said I would adjust to bifocals in a couple of days, I'm not sure I've ever adjusted to them. It is mostly a psychological thing—my way of rebelling.

Can you remember when your hearing started to go? I accused my wife of consciously speaking more softly or turning away from me when she spoke. Even something so simple as walking on a sidewalk at times becomes a challenge. It isn't fun to watch yourself stumble over cracks in the sidewalk. Although we may postpone the aging process, through proper use of the body and by controlling our diet and exercise, we cannot stop it.

You may, if you choose, become angry at God for your failing physical abilities. That doesn't seem like the most productive course of action to take. Being angry at Him does not restore your abilities. You can withdraw from society so no one will see you make age-related mistakes. That too seems like a nonsensical reaction to a natural phenomenon. You can pretend that nothing has changed and everyone is making a big deal out of a nonexistent factor. That may work for a while, but the only person you are really fooling is yourself. Then what can be done? Why not graciously accept the aging process and do whatever you need to do to compensate for the deterioration?

The outward, physical senses are more easily detected by others as they weaken. The private physical functions are more embarrassing. Losing control of bodily functions is not a given. Too many people, because they are embarrassed to admit they are losing control, refuse to be examined by a doctor. Often there are medications that can cure or at least remediate the problem. It could be a bacterial infection causing the incontinence. If so, what a shame to continue to suffer when there is no need. Doctors and exercise physiologists have also been successful at devising exercises to strengthen certain muscles that restore control. Before you decide all as lost, get whatever professional help is available.

If nothing can be done about your private problem, find out how others compensate for the problem and implement their solution. Surely you are not the only one in the world who has had the problem. In the event you are completely unique, you had better believe that a team of doctors somewhere will want to take you on as a research project to find a cure for your condition. Either way, you are a winner.

Sometimes our reflexes slow down before we realize it has happened. Insurance companies readily admit that at a certain age the likelihood of an accident due to the slowing of the reflexes is markedly increased. Although we need not become a self-fulfilling prophecy by automatically accepting the national norm as applying directly to us, it is helpful to read articles on what we can expect as our bodies age.

Some of the more concerning changes happen when we begin to lose our memory. The jokes are endless about seniors standing on the stairs being questioned by a child as to where they are going. They answer that they can't remember whether they were just upstairs coming down or whether they were downstairs going up. If it weren't so real, one might be tempted to laugh. Be conscious when people accuse you of repeating yourself. Again, a doctor's physical exam with some blood work might reveal a hormone deficiency that can be cured by medication. If so, it would be senseless not to take advantage of modern medicine. If there is nothing to be done, you can go into a quiet, sullen depression, although it wouldn't be productive. You could learn to laugh at yourself. Humor, applied in appropriate doses, is almost as good as the nonexistent cure.

A cousin of mine visited with us for a week in Hawaii. We are about the same age (over retirement age). I lamented about my "senior moments." She said, "Oh, you are in the 'here after' stage." Not understanding what she was saying, I asked her to explain. She said, "That is when you go into a room and ask yourself, 'What am I here after?'" After a good laugh, we determined that the "here after" was a good phrase to explain our condition.

Because the memory begins to go slowly, it is helpful to ask people to alert you if you are repeating yourself. A good sense of humor at this point is a valuable tool. As a teacher who taught the same subject several times a day, I found by the end of the day, I couldn't remember whether I had taught the students a certain concept or whether I was just getting ready to teach them. A good set of notes helped curb my problem.

It would be easy to become angry and frustrated at the decreased capacity we are experiencing. It is more productive to use your God-given creativity to make the most of the situation. People spend many good hours laughing at the dumb things they say when their tongues gets thick and the words come out jumbled. Even in the advanced stages of memory loss, there may be times when a person is lucid and remembers the exact details of events that transpired years before. "Why can I remember the color of the shirt I wore fifty years ago and can't even remember what I ate for dinner earlier in the evening?" Maybe someday we'll understand the mechanics behind memory. For now, the best we can do is adjust to the change graciously.

Although the above-mentioned experiences are important and need to be addressed, I would like to devote the remainder of the chapter to a different kind of gracious acceptance. I am referring specifically to changes over which we have little or no control.

A young mother came to see me a few years ago who had experienced the unthinkable. Two sons (one an infant and one three years old) had died within two months of each other. On top of that, her husband had abandoned her for a younger woman. I asked her how she was able to cope. She taught me a valuable lesson. She said, "What choice did I have? The disease which took my infant son was beyond my control and beyond medical control. The accident which took my other son was one I could not prevent. My husband was not open to a negotiated settlement. I made the best out of the hand I was dealt and left the justice and equity in the hands of God." What an attitude.

It wasn't so much *what* happened to her that made her unique. It was *how* she chose to cope with the situation. Over the years I have counseled with people who have had similar (most not quite so severe) experiences. Some have withdrawn into a shell of self-pity. They have been sorely put upon by a higher power, and they deserve to spend the rest of their lives depressed. That is a personal choice, but neither they nor the people who associate with them are benefited by their choice.

On occasions, in spite of the best use of good business principles, companies go under. It isn't a punishment from God for some sin you are unaware of. It may be just the result of being in the wrong place at the wrong time when all the mitigating factors lined up against you. Life still goes on. I read with a degree of disbelief of people who jumped off buildings or otherwise destroyed themselves when the "Crash of 1929" occurred. Couldn't they have started over and built another financial kingdom for themselves? Many of these people were not nearing retirement. They were young enough to fall on their faces financially several times before they really had to be concerned about retirement.

It isn't pleasant to be required to lower your standard of living. Perhaps you may be required to sell your home and acreage and buy a more modest tract home in a lower-class neighborhood. You may find that your neighbors in the new area are real people with dreams just like yours. They may actually be more neighborly than your previous neighbors in the higher-class area. Robbing a bank, or embezzling funds, or forging checks is hardly a mature method of resolving your dilemma. Graciously accepting your plight and then, within accepted bounds, starting over again, may actually result in a larger financial kingdom than you previously enjoyed.

Just at the time in life when you have enough money to be able to enjoy yourself, your health may begin to fail. Bitterly accusing God of dealing unfairly with you is counterproductive at best. If cures are available, you still have some viable options. If the diagnosis is that your condition is terminal, why not accept the inevitable and live life to the fullest?

I have often questioned the practice the medical profession engages in of predicting how long you have left to live. I wonder if we become self-fulfilling prophecies. When they tell you that you have six months to live, do we unconsciously set our mental clock to expire in six months? If they thought you had six months and they told you that you had five years, would it make a difference how long you lived?

Like you, I have encountered many people who are living on borrowed time. Their doctors are amazed that they are still alive years after the projected death date. What makes the difference? Sometimes the will to live is so strong that the body fails to read the latest medical predictions. Although adjustments may have to be made in the daily schedule, there is no need to resign yourself to an early death if you feel you can still carry on.

When the diagnosis is that you will eventually lose your mental facilities, take full advantage of the time before that happens. If the brain works anything like the other muscles of the body, it can forestall mental shutdown only by rigorously exercising the mind. If I ever get to the position where my mind goes, I will know I've given it my best shot at trying to keep it strong and alert. Watching television is said to require less mental energy than sleeping. If that is true, we are doing ourselves a great disservice by gluing ourselves to "the tube" too many hours a day.

There are personal and family histories to write, personal letters to send to close and distant relatives, visits to make, relationships to shore up, and a pastime that is growing in popularity—searching out our family roots—and thousand other things which make watching television pale when compared to their comparative importance. Sometimes we may not even want to do some of these activities, but once started, the task becomes not only enjoyable but also highly motivating.

It may be your lot in life to lose either your eyesight or your hearing. As difficult as the prospects are, if there is nothing you can do about it, you would be better off to make whatever compensating changes you can make. I work with one of the most incredible men I've ever met. He is totally blind, but you would never know it. He goes on trips, navigates the halls, and enjoys life to the fullest. I even heard that when a bus driver became disoriented in Mexico, this man gave verbal directions on how to find the major route using his braille road map. This was after the "seeing" passengers failed to get the bus driver oriented. He has an uncanny sense of direction. His memory is like a steel trap. He has compensated in miraculous ways for the loss of his sight. Occasionally I'll hear people wish out loud that they could be like him.

Dr. Stephen W. Hawkins, a world-renown physicist, was totally immobilized from degenerative muscular dystrophy. People devised a computer program to help him speak so he could continue to bless the world with his remarkable mind. It seemed for Dr. Hawkins the old adage "Where there's a will, there's a way" was more than just a cutesy saying.

I have seen paintings done by artists who had to hold the brush between their teeth because they didn't have use of their arms and hands. I am embarrassed that even with the full use of both of my limbs, I can't come even close to duplicating their efforts. I don't claim to understand the power of the human will, but one cannot deny that it has incredible power.

Perhaps the spectrum of examples I have cited are sufficient to give you a feel for what I am referring to. However, there is one more area that you may want to seriously consider before the circumstance arrives. I am referring to the inevitability of death. In chapter 12, I will discuss in detail a counter-proposal to suicide, either doctor assisted or self-inflicted. In this chapter the concept of "life-support" will be our next area of focus.

Mental pictures are still vivid in my mind of seniors in a vegetative state, hooked up to a series of tubes and monitors to keep them alive. It seems obvious that death is inevitable no matter what medical science can do. In talking with a number of senior citizens about the approach of death, there seems to be some confusion about what their options are short of taking their own lives.

I like the concept of a living will, a written statement directing what your family is to do in the event you become mentally or physically incapable of deciding for yourself. After discovering that such an instrument exists—it can be either written or verbal in the presence of witnesses—I decided that was the right route for me. While, as you will discover in chapter 12, I do not ascribe to the idea of taking authority over that which God has not given me power, I do believe that I am under no special Divine mandate to prolong life when the prognosis for recovery or an acceptable quality of life is not there. Therefore, I have made it clear to my wife and children that, in the event of a serious accident or life-threatening disease where total recovery is not a possibility, they are not to hook me up to life support.

I do believe in doctors and medication and using whatever wisdom I have been blessed with to avoid pain and to enjoy good health as long as possible. Then given the fact that I have exhausted every possible avenue for relief, I have decided to graciously accept the inevitable. At this point in a person's life, some serious introspection is necessary. How prepared are you to meet your Maker? How complete is your understanding of the life that follows this one? Are there last-minute course corrections that, if made, would ease your mind about facing eternity?

I hate to see a person approach death in a panic. As in every other area of life, if you are adequately prepared, the fear of the unknown is greatly lessened. Do you remember the first day on your life's career? Wasn't there some anxiety or even fear? It probably wasn't because you were incapable of performing the tasks required of you as much as the fact that you had never done them before. After a few days or weeks on the job, I would surmise that the fear and anxiety were completely gone. In fact, there probably wasn't a justifiable reason for you to have had the fear in the first place.

Passing from this life to the next is very much like that first day at work. We may fear the unknown, not because we are not prepared but because we do not know exactly what will be required of us. Unfortunately, for us, not many have the opportunity of returning from the next life to tell us what it is like. The number of books that have been written about "near-death" experiences suggest that death is not something to be feared.

As you have been the anchor of stability in the lives of your children and grandchildren, your calmness in approaching the inevitable will also give them the courage to let you depart without undue mourning. They may question their ability to continue life without you. Your experience with the death of your parents or loved ones in the past may put you in a unique position to help allay their fears. I didn't know if I could continue on without my grandfather who had been my substitute father for almost my entire life. His passing was difficult for me because I didn't want to let him go. But to my surprise, as you have all discovered, life did go on. I still treasure the memories we created together. I still draw daily on the lessons he taught me about how to succeed in life. I still miss hearing his laugh and feeling his reassuring arm around my shoulders, but life does go on.

If it hadn't been for the reassuring words of many of my loved ones as they prepared to depart, the parting would have been infinitely more difficult. As you graciously accept the inevitable approach of death, you may have a more profound influence on your family and loved ones than you have ever had in your life. If you were to exhibit terror rather than serenity, you may compound the problems associated with adjustment for your family. Since "inevitable" means "incapable of being avoided or evaded," we ought to be consoled with the knowledge that it is not what we are going to go through but how we will react to death's approach that makes the real difference. We can either make it a pleasant, anticipated event or a nightmare.

I can think of no greater compliment at your passing than for your family and loved ones to say that you lived great and died with dignity. The decisions you make now while death is still some distance off will determine whether you will approach the inevitable with confidence and serenity. Take whatever steps are necessary to put your life in order in preparation for your last, great moment of mortal glory—your passing into eternity.

Chapter 11

"ALL THAT I HAVE"—WILLS AND ESTATES

When looking into the garage that is packed so full of accumulated treasures that there is no room for the car, one begins to wonder if we are part of the "pack-rat" family. Storage sheds are so full of priceless antiques that we couldn't get to them, if we needed them, even if we knew they were there. Although the previous two statements are true in the lives of so many people, much of what you have accumulated through your labors really is of value to your children and grandchildren. Some of the value is sentimental—which is a very valuable consideration. Much of the value is monetary. Priceless antiques command a high price when sold in antique shops, consignment stores, or at flea markets. Sometimes grandchildren cannot afford new (or even used) items that we consider "necessities" as they begin their married lives.

Often what we take for granted because "it's been around forever" is an unspeakable treasure for those who do not have resources to purchase such an item. During your lifetime, you may find that a systematic "going through" your belongings and distributing them to whichever child or grandchild you designate is a rewarding activity. To see the joy and total amazement in their eyes when you give them some prized article will probably be worth more than the item cost you originally. What may seem like junk to you may be a treasure to them. When you are ready to part with some of your goods, let the children and grandchildren decide whether they want them. If they decide they do not want something, there is always a local charity or the Salvation Army center who could find a needy recipient for your excess possessions.

Having been a land surveyor for years, I have been embroiled in some of the most ugly, divisive family battles one can imagine. The general cause was a loving parent saying, "Oh, I don't think I have enough to make a will. I'll just let the kids decide after I'm gone." Sounds really good. You have just created a situation that could potentially destroy that which you have worked a lifetime to accomplish—family unity.

In an earlier chapter I mentioned mediating a family feud over land. It would have been much easier if Mom and Dad had sat down before their health (mental and physical) had eroded and carefully thought through the disposition of their properties. Then employing an attorney, they could have had a will drawn up designating exactly what their (the owners') wishes were for disposing of their property.

Amazing as it sounds, some children resist their parents making out a will. It is like the children do not want to face the eventuality that their parents may not be around forever. "Oh, Mom, there's no hurry on drawing up a will. You've got many years ahead of you!" While that statement may be true, it is very unwise and short-sighted. While my wife and I were still in our twenties, we decided to take a trip to the Middle East. At the time (as it is now) it was embroiled in civil unrest. The tour guide suggested that we have a will drawn up in the unlikely event that something should happen to us. He informed us that without a will, the state, not our extended family, would determine what happened to our children. Enough was said. We were not about to give some disinterested third-party judge the say over who became guardians to our precious little girls and what limited assets we had. From that day until now, we have never been without a will. We have, on several occasions, revised the will to include changes in guardianship of children and who would be the administrator of our will.

Generally, an attorney will be able to guide you through the creation of your will. He will ask you to decide who will be the administrator of your will, or in other words, who will oversee the dividing up of your possessions. Sometimes the oldest child is given the responsibility because all of the other children look up to them and respect their position as the firstborn. Other times there is a "natural" among the children who just has a good business head and a way with the other children that may be lacking in the oldest child. At other times an attorney or family friend may be your choice, in order to avoid any possible conflicts between the children. Anyone who you want—who is willing—can be an administrator. You will need to contact them and ask them if they would be willing to act as administrator of your will. Don't take it for granted that they will accept.

Provisions will be written into the will safeguarding your assets from an administrator who may not have as much integrity as you thought that he or she did. I have also seen wills where a specific time period is designated during which the will is to be executed or carried out. It may be something like: "Within four months from the date of my passing, this will is to be executed. Upon failure to comply for other than legal reasons, I designated attorney so and so as the replacement administrator and order him to execute said will within the next thirty days." The wording may vary, the timing may be tailored to your specific wants, but it is your will being carried out.

Designating a specific time period for completion keeps the process from dragging on endlessly. The longer the execution period, the more likely the heirs are to disagree. The tighter your will, the more likely there will not be feuds over specific items. If you care to assign specific items to specific individuals, you may do so. You may also designate the method used to distribute the goods. For example: "It is my will that the name of each article to be distributed be put on a slip of paper. Fold each paper so the item's name is not visible. Starting at the oldest and proceeding to the youngest, each member of the family is to draw a single slip of paper. Continue in this manner until all pieces of paper are drawn. If, after all papers are drawn, any one or all of the children want to trade items, it is their privilege. No force or coercion is to be used. The original drawing constitutes the transferal of legal ownership to that individual. If they care to sell, give away, or otherwise dispose of the item, it is their uncontested right to do so." Again, the wording may be changed to suit your desires.

You may not want to go to such an elaborate system. You may simply say: "Here is the list of our possessions and alongside each item is the name of the child or person who is to receive it." That is your will. You may also designate an appraisal of each item by a professional and then designate that each heir gets a certain portion of the total dollar value. It is your will.

A word of caution. If you unfairly (in the eyes of the law) divide your estate, any one of your heirs may challenge your will in court. If one or more challenge the legality of your will, it will require the courts to "probate" your will. Probate is the procedure by which a will is proved to be valid or invalid by the courts. You can readily see that whenever a will is probated, someone other than a family member or friend (a judge) will determine how your properties are to be separated.

One couple I worked with as a land surveyor had a provision in their will that if anyone contested the will, they were to be automatically excluded from the will. I don't know if that would legally stand up in court, but it surely put the heirs (children) on notice that the parents did not want their possessions to be the factor that caused a rift in the family.

You may have insurance policies, bank accounts, investments, savings bonds, stock, and so on that your children are not aware of. Declare them in the will and also where they can be located. If you have a safety deposit box in a local bank or elsewhere, let them know that it exists and where it can be found. Otherwise you can see that they may never locate all of your possessions that you want to leave to them. Let them know where the titles to your properties are stored. If you have debts or outstanding obligations, be sure to give enough information so that those obligations can be met before dispersing the liquid assets of your estate.

You may be able to discern from what I have written so far that drawing up a will is not something you do in a few minutes. Time and consideration now can prevent years of hurt feelings and misunderstandings in years to come. A good attorney will work with you in making sure that your wishes are clearly expressed in your will. It may require several revisions before you feel comfortable with the wording and the content of your will.

What if you have a child who has abandoned the family or one you are not interested in giving part of your inheritance to? It would be inappropriate for me to tell you how to settle your affairs. However, I would like to suggest a few principles for your consideration. Something in the past resulted in "bad blood" between you and your child. Whether he or she was at fault is not the real issue. Do you want to be remembered for your littleness of soul? Sometimes when you have nothing to gain (financially or ego-wise) by forgiving wrongs in the past, the person who has been at odds with you will see the error of his or her ways and a reconciliation can be affected. Harboring hard feelings is not conducive to peace for either of you.

Over the twenty-five years I worked with people in establishing and settling their estates, I saw a pattern. Fathers and mothers who seized the opportunity to show by their unselfishness that they did not want to continue the "cold war" were often rewarded by the offended (offending) child returning to mend the relationships.

On the other hand, those parents who steadfastly insisted that the child be excluded from the will perpetuated their hatred for the child for another generation as the time came for the settling of the estate. When the "black sheep" of the family came to the meeting with his or her brothers and sisters and discovered they had been entirely cut off from an inheritance, the feelings of hatred increased and often resulted in an ugly scene in the attorney's office. The transfer of those feelings of hatred for the deceased parents to the living (innocent) brothers and sisters who were included in the will was like a revelation from the dark side. In times like those, I wondered if the deceased parents were permitted to look in on the proceeding from the next life and see the devastating effects their unwillingness to effect a reconciliation caused their descendants.

Another consideration is playing favorites. There may be one child who has tended to your needs more than the others. One child may have been easier to get along with than the others. It is a natural inclination to favor one child over the rest. If you are going to do that, consider taking care of your preferential treatment before your will is executed. In other words, while you are still living, you may gift whatever you want to whomever you want. After all, it is yours to give. Although feelings may still exist between children, it is less likely you will be challenged while you are still living. However, if you are beginning to fail mentally, your other children may try to have you declared "mentally incompetent" and therefore freeze your assets until the will is executed.

The way to avoid the problems associated with wills and estates is to start early enough to detect any predispositions among the children that you may need to counter. Many children do not show their true colors until the parents are deceased and they are greedily sitting in the attorney's office waiting for their share of the estate. Then their disregard for their brothers and sisters becomes evident. If you are able to detect such a hidden quality in one or more of the family members, you may counter it by disposing of the majority of your estate before your demise.

Some parents decide to put the name of the intended inheritor on the deed to the property with the provision that they retain full rights of survivorship. That way, the parents have full and uncontested right to the property while they are alive, and the intended child takes possession upon their passing. Check with the local county recorder's office or an attorney who deals in land transactions to find the best way for your particular case. However you decide to do it, if you wait until too close to your passing date, you increase the likelihood that someone in the family will contest your will.

You may decide that part of your estate is to go to a church or charity or a research institution or an educational institution. It is yours to give, and you have the freedom to designate your assets to whomever you please. Without serious contemplation, you may overlook a person or institution who could greatly benefit from your generosity.

Different states have different laws concerning inheritance. Check with an attorney and find out if there are restrictions or guidelines of what you can do with your estate. None of us are comfortable with how the government has encroached into our personal lives, but barring a major revolution, conditions are not likely to change before your death. My strongest caution is don't try to beat the system. As angry as you may become at the part of your estate that is eaten up by the courts and in attorney fees, if that is what is mandated by state law, you will be better off in the long run complying rather than trying to do an end run around the law.

Multitudes of considerations that have to do with taxes levied against your estate must be addressed if you want to avoid problems for your children. It seems like the system is set up so that no one becomes wealthy without sharing their wealth with the government. When selling agricultural lands, you need to be doubly cautious if you had designated your farm ground as a "greenbelt" earlier. As you sell or dispose of it, your heirs may have to pay taxes on the ground as sub-dividable land or even as commercial property. If you haven't done your research, the taxes may exceed the value of the property. I don't know of an easy way to alert you to the hidden ways that taxes can erode your sizable estate to almost nothing. Taking the time now to investigate the matter may save countless dollars later.

Other possessions that are not as monetarily valuable as land and property, but may have even a greater value to your heirs, should not escape your attention. Family records and histories become our link with the past. The old family Bible that has been handed down in the family from generation to generation may be priceless. If one child is really interested in family traditions and history and the others are not, it would seem reasonable to award them the legacy that you have received from your ancestors.

There may be other articles that have special significance to certain children that may not be important to others. My wife asked for a tea cup from her grandmother's estate. No one in the family cared about or wanted the old cup. So many memories were tied up in the old cup for my wife that she cried big tears when she got the cup. No one but her could appreciate why that cup was so special. Some items are small and insignificant. Others are larger and have a greater monetary value. Be fair and equitable but also be sensitive to sentimental attachment. The old family piano came to me. Only my younger sister and I play the piano, but it was more important to me. That didn't become a divisive issue when my mother passed. I have had it for over half a century. If it meant the difference between a good relationship with my sister, I would have surrendered the piano immediately.

Old pictures and movies can, with a little cost and not a lot of inconvenience, be duplicated so everyone can have their own copy. Many modern inventions make it possible to duplicate priceless treasures; it is no longer an absolute necessity to gift them to a single heir.

When your conscious goal is to divide your earthly possessions in a way that creates unity, you will find that many factors that you may not have considered before will come to mind. If you take adequate time to make a rough draft, then "sleep on it" for a few weeks, then review what you have done, you may prevent overlooking important items.

After you have finalized your will, you may want to invite the children (or heirs) individually to look it over and offer whatever suggestions they feel necessary. After everyone has had a chance to add input into the will, you alone must decide what you will put in and what you will not. By introducing each potential heir to the contents of the will, it takes away the surprise factor. No one will be totally floored when they see that someone else got a certain tract of land or a certain possession. After you finalize your will, if you want to, you can inform each potential heir of your final decision and ask for their understanding and cooperation. Again, your openness will disarm the potentially explosive confrontation when the estate is settled.

Just as you have worked all your life to acquire worldly possessions to enhance your happiness, you do not want to have those same possessions destroy the happiness of your family when you are gone. No amount of physical wealth in the world is worth the destruction of loving relationships between brothers and sisters. You can prevent (or at least lessen the possibility of) that happening by taking action now.

To say, “Oh, I’ll just let the kids fight it out,” is likely to become a prophecy you do not want to be fulfilled. One of the greatest manifestations of love a parent can demonstrate toward their children is to help them enjoy the fruits of their labors. It isn’t too late; if you haven’t done it already, contact an attorney and get the ball rolling. Can you handwrite your own will? Yes, and it may be as valid as one prepared by an attorney. However, legal loopholes are less likely to be found in a will prepared by an attorney. Close up the loopholes, pay the money, and let your mind be at peace knowing that this is just one more important area where you are totally prepared when your summons comes from the next life.

Chapter 12

PREPARING CHILDREN AND GRANDCHILDREN FOR THE FUTURE

It is true that no one lives long enough to make all the mistakes in the world. Unfortunately, it is also true that many fail to learn from their own and the mistakes of others. It has become an alarming trend for seniors, when faced with the prospects of a painful exit from mortality to take the "easy way out." Doctor-assisted suicides together with unassisted suicides among the aging are becoming factors not dealt with in former generations to the degree we are facing them now.

Why not end it all if the prospects are bleak for the rest of your mortal life? If you were an island to yourself (which none of you are) suicide might be a possibility. Let's consider just a few reasons for enduring the pains of mortality over taking the easier, self-determined method of exiting.

By this time in your life, you have established a legacy of endurance. From the very beginning, life has not been easy. Few people were born with silver spoons in their mouths. Even fewer made it through their adolescent years without some pain and suffering, whether it was physical or mental. Marriage was not as easy as Hollywood portrays. Bearing and rearing children probably caused as much suffering as anything you experienced. The adversities of middle age and making a living were seldom as smooth as you may have originally anticipated. Letting the children leave home for college, marriage, travel, or to establish a life of their own may have been more difficult than you previously calculated. Sometimes the loneliness of old age provides too much time to think about how life should have been, focusing on what didn't go right rather than on the joys and good times.

The future is always uncertain. The "what if's" in life can challenge even the most stout-hearted. What if I become senile? What if I become totally bedridden? What if my financial support isn't sufficient to see me to the end? What if I become a burden on my children? The list is endless if you fall into the trap of building bridges across chasms that, when we arrive at the bridge, we find there is no chasm there at all.

Now let's go back and start our trek through life over again. When you were very young, who did you look to as a pillar in your life? Yes, parents play a great part, but what about grandparents? I remember seeing my grandparents (who were probably in their sixties) and thinking that people just couldn't live to be that old. But they were happy, stable people. My mom was harried and stressed because of the burden of raising five children without a mate. Grandma and Grandpa always seemed to have time to talk with me. They were interested in my school projects. They listened as I described the games I played in, the musicals put on by the school, the friends I had, the dates I went on, and the list goes endlessly on. In retrospect, they probably weren't that interested in what I said or did as much as they were interested in me. Are you that anchor for your grandchildren and other young people who associate with you?

I remember suffering an athletic injury and wanting to give up because life wasn't fair and the pain and suffering certainly wasn't worth it. My grandparents encouraged me to keep going, assuring me that the injury would heal and I would play again. They were right. I remember going to the hospital and seeing my grandmother there after a serious stomach operation. I could tell from the tubes and monitors and the look on her face that she was suffering intense pain. She never complained but successfully shifted the conversation to what I was doing. Her example of enduring pain and suffering provided an example for me that I have used my entire life.

Grandpa counseled me through the difficult times of trying to decide what I wanted to do for a living. He was not a highly educated man, but his stories (both personal and of his friends) provided rich food for thought in helping me make my decision. His reassuring anchor statement "My boy, everything will work out all right. Let life unfold naturally" calmed my troubled heart many times. I don't know what I would have done had he not been there.

Remember the time when, as a young couple, you began your family? How excited you may have been to learn you would be parents for the first time. As the delivery approached, I remember (as a young prospective father) worrying about what would happen if my wife and the baby died during the delivery. Then I worried about what I would do if my wife died and left me with the baby. As the delivery approached, I couldn't understand how my wife could be so joyfully looking forward to the ordeal of labor and delivery. It wasn't (for me) a pleasant experience to vicariously experience her pain and suffering. There wasn't anything I could do to make it easier. I hurt mentally as much as she did physically. After what seemed like an eternity, the delivery was over. Almost immediately my wife forgot the pain and suffering and was totally thrilled with the new arrival. I wasn't so quick to forget. I vowed we would not have any more children. Five more children followed the first. Each time I promised "this will be the last." Each time my wife would point out the disparity between the "little" suffering she did and the joy each child brought. Each time I was forced to admit she was right.

What would have been the result if you two had refused to endure the suffering and pain associated with childbirth? What joys would you have missed? What learning and growing experiences would you have forfeited? What memories would you now lack in your memory bank? What quality of life would you have missed if you had misplaced your priorities and opted for the easy, painless life?

When we took our first daughter to see Grandpa and Grandma for the first time, I described the labor and delivery ordeal. Grandpa and Grandma exchanged understanding glances, and then Grandma told about her four children's births (only three lived). No pain-killing drugs, no modern monitors, no sterile environment, just a mid-wife and a bed in the family home. By the time she finished recounting her experiences, we realized how easy we had it compared to them. Of course, everyone in their day did the same thing, but somehow my generation seemed to forget that we weren't the first ones ever to have children.

Remember the worries about having enough money and worldly goods to survive? You may have worked, fretted, stewed, and spent hours trying to figure out how to make the money last to the end of the month.

Through some miracle you made it and eventually probably came out on top. Your grandchildren live in a time when a starter home is going to cost far in excess of $250,000. They are sure they can never make it. What a reassuring thing for them to hear that you had the same fears when your first house cost far less than one-tenth of what theirs will cost. As you laugh and reminisce with them, a feeling of calm will come over them. The mood will change from "we'll never be able to make it in life" to "if Grandpa and Grandma did it, so can we." You bless their lives in so many ways even if you can't afford to give them a dime.

Remember the pain you felt when a child was injured or ran away from home or strayed from the family values? You thought your heart would break, but it didn't and you survived. Now your children and grandchildren are facing the heartache of their children getting into gangs, going into prostitution to support a drug habit, dropping out of society, joining militant anti-government groups or the escalating terrorist organizations. Without your stabilizing counsel, the parents of these wayward children may erroneously believe they are the only ones to suffer such tragedies. You survived the ordeal and have lived long enough to perhaps see your children or grandchildren come back into the mainstream of life. How many "hippies" of the early sixties do you see still running around taunting "free love," drug abuse, social irresponsibility, and so on? Most of them grew out of their rebellious stage and are responsible adults. You may even have been numbered among that group.

Now you have arrived at the point in life where your posterity has never been. You have lived long enough to see that there is purpose in suffering. You have learned some lessons for survival that do not change with the changing of the calendar. You are in a unique situation to make a significant difference. There is no doubt that you are probably tired and wonder if you are equal to this final battle of failing health as you approach death. Since when is this approach any different than all the others mentioned above? Considered in the proper light, this is just another challenge in a long line of challenges you have faced and successfully overcome from the day you were born.

There is an added responsibility that falls on your shoulders as the patriarch or matriarch of the extended family. What is the legacy and example you will leave for those who follow you? Will you, by your example, teach them that when things get tough you avoid the pain and suffering by taking your own life? Will a granddaughter who discovers she is pregnant out of wedlock use you as an example for jumping in front of a car and ending it all? Will a grandson look to you when he has just been busted for possession of illegal drugs, steal his father's pistol, and end his own life? You may not be able to prevent them from taking drastic action, but there certainly isn't any benefit associated with your legitimizing it.

If you stop to consider the tremendous impact you have had on your family (think about the impact your grandparents may have had on you), you will readily see you owe it to yourself and those who follow you to endure the pains of this life for a higher cause than your own personal comfort. I am not suggesting that your suffering will be any less. It may be the most difficult suffering you have endured in your life. Childbirth was also the most difficult suffering you had endured in your life to that point, and you made it through. Why? Because you realized the joys and blessings that would result from your suffering.

What could possibly benefit you to suffer until death? All four of my grandparents have long since died. All four suffered more than I would have chosen for them if I had been in control. Their hundreds of posterity all look to them as examples of enduring the trials of life. Not one of their offspring (to this point) has taken his or her own life, although several have been in pretty bleak circumstances. "If Grandpa and Grandma could do it, so can I" is a common phrase when we get together and consider the problems we are facing.

You may wonder what personal benefit you will derive from your continuing to endure the pain and suffering that lies ahead. Without turning theologian, it is difficult to talk about life after death (the subject of a later chapter). However, for Christians one scripture will help bring into focus what all of us must face with the eye of faith: "Though he were a Son, yet learned he obedience by the things that he suffered; and being made perfect he became . . . " (Hebrews 5:8–9). What Christ became because of His suffering was unique to Himself. What God intends for you and me to become may be equally as unique. However, the Savior qualified to become the "author of eternal salvation" by the things that He suffered. If we follow His divine invitation, "Come and follow me" (Matthew 19:21), we will not, indeed cannot not, shrink when our greatest trial comes. It will require a vision enhanced from the next life to understand the magnitude and long reaching benefits that will come to each individual who successfully endures to the end even though it is painful and distasteful.

Some face death after having lost all consciousness of their physical surroundings. How could existing in a vegetative state possibly benefit them? It may be that the greatest benefit of their continued existence is not for them personally but for those who are afforded the opportunity of meeting their needs. As we sacrifice to help those whose minds have rendered them incapable of even recognizing their family, or knowing what day of the week it is, or even knowing what time of the day it is, we grow and learn. Service to our fellow beings brings its own joy even if they are incapable of acknowledging our service or responding to it.

Again, look back to your past. Why do you have such an intense love for your children? Is it not because you sacrificed your own personal needs and desires to meet theirs? Perhaps only in that kind of selfless sacrifice can people learn to love others more than they love themselves. We love those for whom we sacrifice. Why deprive your loved ones of the opportunity to develop that kind of God-like love?

It may be that we provide the very opportunities our children and grandchildren need in order to fine tune and polish their abilities to empathize and sympathize. They may be able to learn in no other way how to subject their own selfish desires for a higher cause than in caring for the needs of others. It may be through the financial sacrifices they may be required to make for you that they learn how to love others more than they love themselves. It may be in their required sacrifices to meet your daily needs they are forced to slow down long enough to reconsider the direction their lives are taking and make whatever mid-course corrections are necessary. It may be that their daily ministrations to you helps them put priorities on their lives that they otherwise would not have done. With a little effort, this list of benefits to those who will care for you can be expanded to fill an entire volume. The truly loving thing to do is to patiently provide the situation where your children and grandchildren can develop those refined human qualities of love that can be developed in no other way than through service.

Consider the parents and brothers and sisters of a mentally disabled baby. I have never met such a family who said the sacrifice was not worth it. Ask around if you question my thesis. It is only those who have never had a handicapped child who make comments like, "Wouldn't it have been better if he had died at birth?" or "I feel so sorry for your family having to make so many sacrifices for this deformed human being!" If you want to be put in your place or even receive a verbal thrashing, just try one of those statements or a similar one on the family of a disabled child.

I hope you'll excuse yet another personal example. For almost forty years after my father died, my mother and grandparents hardly ever mentioned his name. Because he had some problems with his personality and behavior that were embarrassing to the family, mention of him was just not a regular occurrence. My mother and grandparents are wonderful people. They made a decision, whether consciously or unconsciously, that they would not share that part of our lives with us. It was a unilateral decision, made for us without consulting us. In early 1990 we started asking questions about my father. The doors of the memories of my mother and grandparents were swung open. Information that had been hidden from us was revealed. I really appreciate knowing even some of the very painful facts about my father. At last he became a real person rather than just a name. I could then have elected to learn no more if I had chosen, but the choice would have been mine to make.

The point I make is this: You act in an unintentionally selfish mode when you decide for people something they can and should decide for themselves. I would like to have had the option of learning of my father when I was much younger. But my elders didn't volunteer, and I was naive enough not to ask; the thought never crossed my mind. When you decide to deprive your children and grandchildren of your presence by taking your own life, aren't you acting in a very selfish, unilateral way? Even if they were to come to you and encourage you to end it all, would you be acting responsibly knowing that you have so much to give in spite of the deterioration of the body?

If the wise are all taken from our midst, who will provide the stability in times of crisis? If you, our link with the past, is removed, how will we perpetuate the traditions and values of our fathers? If children do not learn to sacrifice for the benefit of others, will our society self-consume in the mire of self-centeredness? If we leave a legacy of faltering when faced with the great challenges of life, will we be remembered as the ones who gave license to those who followed to shrink back from the battle? Will those who follow lose the freedoms we now enjoy because they have never learned to stand firm in the face of insurmountable odds? Will our future world be built on the foundation of running away from painful challenges?

You hold the key to reversing the current trend. Doctors, now being examined in the courts of law, try to justify their actions by saying they are trying to eliminate suffering. In light of your expanded vision, would you say that eliminating individual suffering at the expense of the entire society developing habits that will help us avoid destruction was really eliminating suffering? The doctors say, "We are doing it for the benefit of the patient." Are they? What if, as the author of Hebrews suggests, we are perfected by suffering? Are those well-intended but mis-directed doctors actually robbing us of blessings in the next life that they (and we) have no concept of? There is too much at stake to chance that death ends our existence. There is too much evidence pointing to the fact that the spirit of man continues on after the body is discarded. There is too much riding on our setting an example of faithful endurance in the face of impossible odds for us to take the easy way out.

I wonder if suicide, whether doctor-assisted or by our own hands, represents a flaw in our professed faith in God. It seems that God ordained death as the means of releasing our spirits from our bodies when the bodies become untenable tabernacles for our spirits. Has God just plain lost control over when we die? Do we need to help Him decide when the time is right for us to pass from mortality to immortality? Are we afraid that God will allow us to suffer beyond that which would be for our own good and our eternal welfare? Do we think that God has so many children that He doesn't have time to consider each individual's needs?

When a doctor or anyone else decides to take the power of God, who dictates the time of death, into his or her own hands, are we not making a grave mistake? The ancient prophet Isaiah reminded us that God does not see, think, or reason as man does. He said, "For my thoughts are not your thoughts, neither are your ways my ways, saith the Lord. For as the heavens are higher than the earth, so are my ways higher than your ways, and my thoughts than your thoughts" (Isaiah 55:8–9).

Without being burdened by the facts nor hindered by eternal vision, many people (doctors included) will draw conclusions from their restricted mortal vision, and make decisions that have eternal implications. I, for one, want to raise a voice and say, "Let God be God, and let's you and I be content to be His children." I firmly believe, having watched suffering all my life and certainly not having been exempted myself, that there is divine purpose in all of it. I have watched peace come to the physically tormented at the time of death. I have heard the final declarations of those who have endured to the very end. Theirs is not the voice of regret for having suffered the pains of mortality. Theirs is unanimously the voice of thanksgiving that they had the privilege of living life to the very end. They are not prone to want to continue the fight. They willingly reach up and take the hand of God and depart for the next world firm in the faith that the crosses they have born in mortal life will be to their benefit in the world to come.

One final thought before ending this chapter. Do you need to prolong life when the prognosis for recovery is not there or the possibility of a quality type of life in the future is non-existent? That is a question each individual must answer. My conclusion is no. Since it was God who ordained death as the means of releasing the spirit from the body, I see nothing in the Holy Bible or in the theology of the churches that suggest that we must cling to mortal life longer than the natural processes of life would normally keep us here. Said more succinctly: We must not take the power of God into our own hands and end our lives, but we need not resist the power of God to release our spirits from our bodies when He dictates that our time has come.

My living will states that my spouse and children are not to hook me up to life support if there is little or no chance of full recovery. Without wanting to overuse the title of the book, you can readily discern that I harbor a very strong belief that we should "live until we die" and then graciously accept death as part of the divine plan for mankind.

Chapter 13

LEARNING FROM THE PAST

Why do we teach history in our schools? Is there so little to learn that we must spend so much time studying the past? To one who is unschooled, it may seem that an inordinate amount of time is spent rehashing the lives of people who have been dead longer than anyone now alive can remember. However, observed more closely, you will discover that some things never change. Yes, the dress, the conditions in which they lived, even their way of talking may be very antiquated by our standards. However, the principles that contributed to their success then are the same today.

Does history repeat itself? I'm not sure. But one thing is certain—the principles behind the problems that they faced are no different than the ones we face. As we read the accounts of people who lived in England many years ago under tyrannical kings, it strikes a familiar chord with some of the conditions under which we live. How did they survive? If we can discover that, we will have a valuable key to help us survive.

One does not have to look back hundreds of years to find examples of heroes and heroines. Young people today need only to look to *you* for inspiration in meeting the challenges of life. If you were to ask them, many of the young people would classify you as being "living history." We laugh at what they call "old," but compared to them, we probably are. Why not take full advantage of your status, even if you feel it has been unjustly bestowed?

Oral (spoken) history can be a powerful motivator. Although psychologists and family therapists caution us against such phrases as "When I was your age" or "In my day," not all of those phrases are bad. If you use comparisons to put down or demean the younger people, then I heartily agree that they should not be used. However, when comparisons are used to draw parallels, to teach principles, to help young people avoid mistakes of the past, I disagree that they should not be used. Nothing seems to be good or bad in and of itself (see Romans 14:14 for biblical substantiation of that principle). It is the way we view things and the use we make of them that gives things their relative status. For instance, drugs are not bad if they are used under a doctor's direction to heal the sick. They are "bad" if they are abused and destroy the lives of people. It is in the abuse, not the use of anything that makes it "bad."

How do you approach young people so they will openly welcome your teachings from the past? One method may not be all inclusive. It may require that you use a variety of teaching methods. If you have established a loving relationship, young people are less likely to reject your counsel. Assuming that you have a good relationship already, you might remember that humor is a great way to teach heavy topics in a light way. Laughing at mistakes we made as children or young adults helps young people today realize that, although life is very serious, most mistakes are usually not fatal. As a professional teacher, I used humor every time I felt it was appropriate. If the milieu (the spirit that developed or evolved in the class) was becoming too sullen because of the weight of the topics we were discussing, I tried to lighten it up by using a play on words or even a joke. The laughter that followed was like taking a heavy, dark blanket off from the students' minds. Of course, there are times when making light comments is not appropriate. As it is in the classroom, so it is in your teaching situations. It does not require a doctorate degree to determine when humor can be effectively used.

If you have successfully analyzed your past and isolated certain lessons you learned from your past—whether positive or negative—package them in as interesting language as you possibly can, and try them out on your grandchildren or other young people you associate with. The more time you spend analyzing and evaluating your past, the more convinced you will become that you have experienced every lesson of life that those people written about in history books have experienced. Perhaps your life has not been so dynamic that Hollywood wants to make a movie about it. But you have lived and you have learned and you have experienced.

You may be saying to yourself, "The world these kids face with computers, the worldwide internet, and so on is so foreign to me, I cannot identify with them and they likely cannot identify with me." Not so. Do you remember how scared you were when electronic calculators were first introduced? I thought if I made a mistake that I would short out the calculator and destroy the whole thing. Now I look back and laugh because I understand that, although I may have lost some calculations, the calculator would not allow me to ruin it by the keys I punched. The same principle exists with the computer. We may lose the data we just entered, but we won't ruin the machine.

I can hardly conceive what inventions are on the horizon for the kids. Even if we can't keep up with them, the fear of the unfamiliar is the same whether we are talking about cyberspace or calculators or touch tone phones or early radios. Can you remember before your first airplane flight? I would say for me the emotion was more like terror than fear. Even though I have flown many times, I still get a little tight in the stomach before the plane departs. Helping young people address their fears is one thing that will never change.

I spent a lot of time talking with college students about their irrational fears concerning marriage. One would think this is the first generation ever to be faced with overwhelming challenges as they marry. They seemed almost in a state of denial when I told them my wife and I faced those same fears over five decades ago. As you share with your grandchildren the hopes and fears you experienced as soon-to-be married lovers, they will readily identify with your example. The past is a great teacher for the present and future. When you spark their attention, you had better be prepared to spend a considerable amount of time. Let them draw the parallels between your experience and what they are going through.

Almost daily in the newspaper or on television are stories of tornadoes, flash floods, earthquakes, and hurricanes. Having not lived so many years, the young are likely to think that life is just one huge "flash flood." You have lived long enough to know that the crisis only lasts a few minutes. It is the clean-up that requires the sustained effort. So it is in life. The flash floods would be impossible to handle if they were constant, but they are not. An unprecedented number of young people are taking their own lives. People don't self-destruct because they see multiple positive options for the future. When the gloom and doom that the newscasters often paint—such a dismal picture for the youth—it requires someone with maturity and stability to counteract the depressive spirit that follows. You may be that someone for many people who are struggling because of limited vision of how the past, present, and future interrelate.

I remember when the Korean War started. We all thought the second World War was the war to end all wars. American troops again deployed onto foreign soil. There was almost a blanket of gloom over the country. As the conflict dragged on, spirits dipped even lower. But the end did come and relative peace was re-established. Then came Vietnam. Again, the country was entangled in foreign conflict. History books may give the mistaken impression to the young that the Vietnam War started before the Korean War ended. It requires people who lived during those "ancient days" to put those conflicts into proper perspective. Life, opportunities, marriage, families, careers, schooling, and so on continued even while the wars were raging. Likely there will be national and international conflict for the foreseeable future given the spreading of the terrorist ideology.

After a devastating hurricane in southern Florida (not an unheard-of event), the news media interviewed people whose homes had been destroyed. They had lost virtually every material possession. Surprisingly there was not a feeling of despair and gloom. Rather, the nation was shocked to see and hear the optimism the townspeople exhibited. They were determined to rebuild the town even better than it was before. Good for them! So many young people (and many not so young) wallow in self-pity when they have experienced one of life's flash floods.

We have lived long enough to observe both attitudes played to their logical conclusion. The "wallowers" shrivel up and die. Sometimes they continue to exist physically, but their personality, vitality, drive, attitude, and zest for life have all bottomed out. In contrast, others who experienced the same flash flood immediately sized up the situation, rolled up their sleeves, and started the rebuilding process. No one forces us to look at a situation through pessimistic glasses. Usually, no one smooths out the rough spots. It is not the situation but the attitude that makes the difference.

Everyone can benefit from someone who has been through the trials of life, telling them that the storms will pass and there are some wonderful days ahead. As a teenager I vividly remember a newspaper picture of a bearded, scraggly-looking man walking the streets of Washington, D.C. with a placard that read, "The End Is Near." It scared me a little until I talked with my grandfather about it. He gave a deep belly laugh and told me the doomsayers were saying the same thing when he was my age. Then—and only then—was I able to laugh at the picture.

Young people are likely to count the dollars lost in the flash floods of life. Unless you guide their vision to look, they will likely miss the gold lying all around them. I am not necessarily referring to the gold that is traded in the stock market. I mean the real part of people's character that isn't seen in full until a crisis reveals it. I remember the crash of an airplane in Washington, D.C. when a man literally sacrificed his life helping rescue injured people from the wreckage in the icy Potomac River. I can still see the pained look on the firefighter's face when he realized that the child he had risked his life to rescue from the building bombed in Oklahoma City was dead. Stories of people forgetting themselves in the service of those with a greater need are endless.

As we are bombarded with the accounts of crime, corruption, fraud, embezzlement, and so on, we may find it easy to believe that everyone in the world is totally corrupt. It isn't until the flash floods, tornadoes, earthquakes and tsunamis of life come that we realize that there are a lot of good people out there. You, better than anyone else, are in a position to help the discouraged youth see the silver lining on otherwise very dark clouds of life.

To change directions a little, it is also imperative that we personally learn from the past. There are mistakes we have made, habits we have engaged in for years, ways of doing things that are hurtful to others, and the list goes on. Are we wise enough to learn from the past that these factors work crosswise to our goal of peace and happiness? It requires a mammoth effort to tackle a negative family trait and overcome it. With tremendous effort, it can be done. For example, biting your lip for just a second can be the beginning of gaining control over your explosive temper. Being aware of the problem is a huge step toward solving it. When we ignore a problem or refuse to admit that we have a problem, it only postpones the time when we can overcome it.

My wife and I were at a restaurant awhile ago and saw three women sitting at an adjacent table. It was obvious from the marked family resemblance that this was a grandmother, her daughter, and her granddaughter. They had the same mannerisms, the same way of speaking, and (unfortunately) the same way of handling people. Their order came. In voices loud enough to alert the entire clientele in the restaurant, they each in turn announced that their meal was not fit for a dog to eat. They demanded that the waitress have the cook replace this "garbage" with some good food. I understand that occasionally a cook might not be as professional as some would like, but for all three to have poorly prepared food when no one else in the restaurant had any complaints is somewhat unusual.

Even if their food was ill-prepared, wouldn't it have been more mature to quietly inform the waitress rather than making such a public issue out of such a private mishap? My wife and I ordered, ate, and left before these three women finally got their orders right. It wasn't that the cook was slow. The three women sent portions of each of their next meals back as well! I felt sorry for the women. Not that their food was bad, but because the childishness of the grandmother had been passed on to her daughter, who in turn had conveyed the habit to the next generation. I wondered if there was a little girl at home somewhere who would have been a carbon copy of her three progenitors.

Taking the time to identify and overcome negative family traits may be one of the more productive activities you can engage in. It may also be one of the most appreciated things you can do for society. When you are older, you may speak with authority about things you have experienced firsthand that others may have only read about. From a very early age, you have probably been able to see how ridiculous a fist fight between schoolmates really is. There are no winners. Everyone loses. Even if one boy is successful in subduing the other, friendships are ruined or weakened, classmates are divided as they take sides, pleasant activities have a bitter spirit cast over them, teachers and students are set at odds as they try to "get to the bottom of this," and the list goes on. It doesn't seem that the young have learned this lesson any better than we did. However, I never remember my elders sitting down and explaining the futility of fighting to me. Can you learn from the past and bless the next generation by teaching them to avoid the mistakes of our generation? One thing is certain, if you don't *try* teaching them, you will never succeed. At least if you try, you have a chance for success.

We have lived long enough to see a cycle that defies exception—the "living beyond your means" cycle. The invention of "easy money," "easy credit," "no money down and forever to pay" philosophy sounds too good to be true. We discussed earlier the pitfalls of easy credit. Now focus on the not-so-obvious consequences of getting in debt. Although the media would have you believe that the major cause of marital discord is sexual incompatibility, the truth is that money problems underlie most of the problems we see today. When a husband and wife fail to agree on how to spend the money, it is only a matter of time until there is a rift in their marriage relationship.

It isn't even that there must be a certain way of spending money. There must be unity or there will be hard feelings. Having lived long enough to see recessions and depressions, it is helpful to share your insight with those who are falling into the trap of easy finance. Financial irresponsibility on the part of one or the other in a marriage is just the tip of the iceberg. Lack of communication, lack of trust, lack of maturity, lack of team spirit, lack of truthfulness are all part of the ugly iceberg hidden below the surface. It will require your maturity to help young married grandchildren see that the solution to their financial problems will only be permanent when they address the other issues.

As a people, we are more apt to look at the tip of the iceberg and deny that there is anything underneath it. As mature seniors who have analyzed and thought things through relying upon a lifetime of experience, we are not so quick to implement a cure that does not cover all the contributing factors. If you haven't taken time to look at the outer rings of the ever-expanding circles created when a pebble is dropped into a pond, you might benefit from the exercise. Look back at when you were the sharpest or most cutting with your family. Was it after a hard, frustrating day at work? Have you noticed that life wasn't necessarily happiest when everything was going smoothly? It may have been working together through the tough times that comes to mind when thinking about "the good old days." Have you discovered that you may not have enjoyed life more during the times of prosperity? It may have been that scrimping together as a family, saving for the much-anticipated family vacation, was actually more fun than the vacation. You may have noticed that it wasn't necessarily when everyone was healthy that your happiness level was highest. It may have been when a family member got out of the hospital that everyone talks about as one of the happiest times of your life.

The closing principle for this chapter would be that without contrasts, life cannot be enjoyed to the fullest. Without tasting the bitter occasionally, the sweet has nothing to be contrasted with. Without a few lows, how can you appreciate the highs? Mortal life does not seem to be constructed as a perpetual high. If all we do is focus on the lows, we are apt to miss the view from the peaks. As a senior citizen, you are in the best position of all to help those who erroneously think that life is just one wallowing valley, to see that there are peaks on each side of the valley—or there wouldn't be a valley at all. Peaks and high mountains define valleys. Valleys make it possible for there to be peaks and mountains. Can we learn from the past?

Chapter 14

EVER CHANGING YET NEVER CHANGING

Scientists say that our bodies are in a constant state of change. Skin dies and sloughs off and is replaced by new skin. During the early days of our lives, change was observable almost daily. If you were close to your grandchildren during their first few years, it was almost an amazement how quickly they changed from little babies to toddlers to young children. The reason I focus on your grandchildren is that many parents say they were with their children so much of the time they really didn't observe the changes. It is too bad that we couldn't stand back and realize how quickly our children were changing.

The rapid changes during childhood and adolescence, if we had been more aware, may have been an encouragement when times of discouragement occurred during especially challenging phases of our children's lives. We even had names for some of the phases our children passed through: the terrible twos; the trying threes; the frustrating fours, and so on. At times you may have even wondered if you would survive their teenage years. But, observed or unobserved, the changes took place.

One day, as it seemed, the children were grown and ready to leave home. You may have even been reluctant to let them go since you were sure they were too young and inexperienced to cope with the challenges of life. How could they possibly make it own their own? But in a remarkable contradiction to every projection, they did make it. Amazingly, they may have even done better than we did.

After young adulthood, changes were not so evident. Physical growth had stopped—at least the vertical growth. Horizontal growth may have become a constant battle. It may have seemed that intellectual growth had also greatly slowed, if it didn't completely stop. It may have become a greater challenge to get your brain to retain the information you wanted to remember.

There may have been a time in early adulthood when you thought you would never grow old. Your body was in its prime. You could run, jump, exercise, swim, hike, or do whatever you wanted. Then the body started to change again. This series of changes was not the positive, desirable changes you had experienced during youth. Now sight was beginning to dim, hearing was not so acute, taste buds were not as sensitive, muscles not so powerful, joints not so flexible, and reflexes not so responsive.

The ever-changing part is easy to observe because it is outward. What about the "never changing" part? From early adolescence we were expected to develop and refine interpersonal skills. We had to learn to suppress our own selfish wants for the benefit of others. We learned to be pleasant even when we didn't feel very well. In fact, "not feeling very well" wasn't an excuse for failure to perform.

A friend told of an experience with a teenage boy who had volunteered to help clean up a local park. It was agreed that at a designated time on Saturday morning, they would meet at the town hall and go to the park together. My elderly friend was there at the appointed hour, but the boy did not show up. After waiting for the better part of an hour, my friend went to the park and cleaned by himself. The boy never came.

The next day he chanced to meet the young man at the local church service. He mentioned that he had waited for an hour and then gone to the park himself. The young man hemmed and hawed and then pitifully said, "Well, I really didn't feel very good." Irritated at his immaturity, my friend took the young man by the shoulders and said, "Young man, don't you know that the majority of the work in this world is done by people who don't feel very good?"

I love that statement. If we wait until we "feel good" or until it is convenient, the majority of the opportunities of life will pass us by. If we are where we have committed to be, even when we don't feel very well (of course within reason), we will find that in the doing of the promised task, our bodies actually heal themselves and we feel much better than if we had stayed home and pampered ourselves.

Now, the aging process may be starting to take its toll. It isn't as easy to keep smiling when we aren't feeling very well or when the pain level increases to where we are really uncomfortable. But, if we are going to mark the desired path for those who are following, we must be "never changing." I have never met a person who loves to be around a constant complainer. Often when people get together and tell of their aches and pains, the only reason they quietly listen to others describe their aches and pains is so they have an audience when it is their turn!

However, in spite of increasing aches and pains you may be experiencing, perhaps more now than ever before in modern history, there is a real need for grandparents to get involved in the teaching and molding of the rising generation. If we refuse to help, what will happen to our families in the future? Will we even have a family to pass on the family name?

In *Gabler's Educational Resource Newsletter*, a summary of challenges facing school personnel were reported by public school authorities. They did a comparison between a similar study conducted in 1940 with those facing teachers in 1982. A mere recital of their findings is sobering. In 1940, school principals said the greatest challenges they were facing in dealing with school children were 1) talking, 2) chewing gum, 3) making noise, 4) running in the halls, 5) getting out of turn in line, 6) wearing improper clothing, and 7) not putting paper in wastebaskets.

Compare that list to what was reported as happening in the school just forty-two years later. In 1982 principals and teachers made a list of the most serious problems they were facing in dealing with students. They were 1) rape, 2) robbery, 3) assault, 4) burglary, 5) arson, 6) bombings, 7) murder, 8) suicide, 9) absence, 10) vandalism, 11) extortion, 12) drugs, 13) alcohol, 14) gang warfare, 15) pregnancy, 16) abortion, and 17) venereal disease. If you are able to get your breath after reading that list, I would ask you to consider one more question: What has happened in the public school since 1982? Are we getting a handle on the problems, or are they continuing to escalate? Some question the validity of those reports, but having been an educator for the past forty-plus years, I can attest to the deterioration of discipline and the escalation of problems not only in the public schools but also in society. I'll venture that you share my observations.

You may say, "I'm just too tired to keep going!" There is no question that you have earned the right to take a rest. However, when the family ship is in mid-ocean and has sprung a leak, it is hardly the time to take a vacation. Your "never changing" qualities that have made you an example to be emulated must be made available to the young.

In our day, a mother working outside the home was a rarity; today it is almost a necessity. With the price of housing, transportation, food, clothing, and so on escalating, one income may not be sufficient to meet all the demands. While many companies and even some governmental agencies are providing day care centers for your grandchildren, it is also a reported fact that abuse and neglect in many of these facilities is an appalling reality. During those very impressionable, formative years, children learn to love and trust or to hate and be cynical. If we wait until the teenage years to consciously mold their personalities, it may be everlastingly too late.

While it seems true that today's kids are mouthier and more disrespectful than they were a generation ago, it is not true that all children fall into that category. Some young people are courteous and polite. The difference seems to be the training they received when they were young.

Have you ever heard yourself saying something like, "Why, if I had talked that way to my elders when I was young, it would have required the services of an oral surgeon to put my teeth back in my mouth!"? Where do young people learn what is appropriate and what isn't when dealing with adults and society? Are they to learn it from overworked, understaffed day care centers? If we wait for them to be taught there, it is likely it will never happen. Although it is their parents' responsibility to teach them, the mental and physical fatigue of working all day trying to make a living often leaves them unable to do an adequate job of training their children when they get home.

It could be that you are the only hope the next generation has. Your "never changing" attributes that contributed to the successful society in which we now live is needed like it has never been needed before. So even when it would be nice to sit on the sidelines and watch the game, it may be necessary for you to suit up again and keep on playing.

Is it an obligation you owe your family and society? Yes and no. Let's consider the "no" first. If you were to be summoned into a court of law, the judge would likely acquit you. You would not be sent to prison for not stepping in and helping your children raise your grandchildren. As you have noticed from several recent court cases, the same is not true for parents. Society is rapidly getting its fill of children who are out of control. Parents are now being tried and convicted for not controlling their children's behavior. Fines and even possible imprisonment are being levied against delinquent parents. That will likely never happen to grandparents who are one generation removed.

However, those grandsons will be the ones to carry on the family name. Their actions and behavior directly affect the way people look at your family. One family wrote a sign above the inside of the front door. It reads "Return with Honor." Every time a family member left the house, there was the visual reminder that they would return and must account for the way they conducted themselves. As a young man in that family spoke with me about the sign, he said that his parents had impressed upon him since he was very young that he had an obligation to act in such a way that honor would come to the family. He said that every time he thought about doing something he knew was wrong, he would think about the sign. Although he isn't perfect, he certainly is an honor to the family name.

If both your son and daughter-in-law or your daughter and son-in-law are obliged to work outside the home, who will be there to encourage the grandchildren to "return with honor"? Frequent visits by Grandma and Grandpa can have a greater impact on the grandchildren than you might believe. I don't remember seeing my grandparents very often, but as I reflect on my "significant others" (people who have profoundly influenced my life), both Grandma and Grandpa are on the list. It may not require a full-time commitment on your part. It may require just a more conscious commitment and effort to be there for them.

The "yes" part of the above answer about it being your obligation comes from within rather than from the outside. If your sense of duty and your love of your grandchildren is stronger than your desire to sit back and take it easy, then the answer about it being an obligation to try to influence them for good is "yes."

I have seen grandparents revitalized as they have become more involved in the lives of their grandchildren. Just like going to the park to pick up papers even when "you didn't feel very good" may have resulted in a renewal of your physical strength, so getting involved may rejuvenate your mental, emotional, and physical strength. When you think you have no more to give, remember when you were a young mother or a young father and felt the same way. What choices did you have? If you had given up then, your children would have died because you were the sole source of help in meeting their physical needs. So you kept on going even if you cried a bit and wished it could be otherwise.

Since you already have a proven track record of enduring to the end no matter what the demands on your time and energy were, why not continue without changing? See if there isn't a "second mile" left in you. I would doubt that anyone will stand back and criticize you if you choose to take the easier approach and not get involved, but many people will praise your efforts forever if you choose to get involved. Your children will be grateful beyond expression if you just "drop by and take the kids for an evening" or if Grandpa or Grandma takes a struggling teenager out for an ice cream cone. A walk in the park feeding the ducks does much more good than just keeping the ducks from starving. Asking a wavering grandson to help on a project you really could easily do yourself is more valuable than just getting the project done. The showing up at a ballet or a ball game is of far greater benefit than just having one or two more in the audience. Lives are changed and characters are molded.

Even if no one ever recognizes your efforts and sacrifices, you will know that you have done something positive to help the next generation cope with the super-human challenges they face. There may even be times when you are rebuffed for trying to help. It is easy to become offended when your children or grandchildren tell you they don't need or want your help. But remember to be "never changing." Sometimes pride or lack of vision stand in the way of people graciously accepting help. It often requires that you be the bigger person in knowing when your help is becoming more of a hindrance than a help no matter what you intended.

A lifetime of service has put you in a unique position to help develop an environment of stability in a very unstable world. Have times really changed that much, or are we just not doing as well at passing the tests as we did a generation ago? The answer to that question is not readily evident. There were people in 1940 who engaged in almost all of the activities on the 1982 list, although fewer. Today, many young parents and their children seem to have lost heart for the battle. This may be where your "never changing" attitude is priceless. Can a person negotiate the storms of life without being shipwrecked on the hidden shoals? You are a living testimonial that it can happen.

If there was a way of making a stronger plea to be constant and never changing in the characteristics you have developed over a lifetime, I would use it. So as your body continues to change in a way that is not always desirable, make sure you continue to hold fast to those qualities that have made you an anchor to your family and friends during these troubled times.

Chapter 15

LIFE AFTER LOSING A MATE

Nothing seems more difficult than adjusting to the loss of a mate. This is particularly true if you have been married a long time or were particularly close to the spouse. It is not uncommon to go through stages of numbness, denial, anger, and sometimes despondent resignation after the funeral. There have been some wonderful books written about the grieving and healing process after death. My intent is not to rehash old teachings but to consider in a fresh light the opportunities that lie ahead of you.

Is there life after losing a mate? The answer depends on you. For many, life takes on a new, even richer dimension after the funeral. For others the answer is a sullen "no." As with so many other principles mentioned in this book, your attitude is the determining factor. I have seen widows cling to the closed casket, frantically pleading for the deceased to return. It hasn't ever happened when I have been a witness. Other people have, with quiet dignity, accepted the death as a vitally important part of life. If you haven't been faced with the situation yet, take some time and talk it over with your spouse. Take control of your life and determine how you want to react when the time comes or how you hope your mate will react if you should pass on first.

Understanding that there will be stages or phases you will pass through ranging from depression to anger to acceptance, we will leave that to the other authors who have written extensively on the subject. Let us turn our attention to some areas they may not have fully investigated.

One consideration is the family and friends at the funeral. Although you may be in more intense mental pain than you have ever experienced, could you actually lessen your pain by focusing on the needs of others at the funeral? I was only four and a half when my father passed away. I don't remember anything about the funeral service except that my mother was standing by the open casket greeting mourners as they passed by for a final goodbye with my father. I don't remember her crying or sniffling out of control. I remember her comforting those who came through the line. Here was a young widow faced with the overwhelming task of raising five children between the ages of eleven and three years. She had no formal education or a career to fall back on. Help from her family or her in-laws was not likely to come—and it didn't! All of this must have been weighing on her mind, but she (as she always had been) focused on easing the burden of those who came to comfort.

In the subsequent deaths of her father and mother, her father-in-law and mother-in-law, her second husband, three of her brothers, her beloved sister-in-law, a daughter, and a multitude of friends (when you're over ninety these things happen), my mother exhibited the same stabilizing influence. I have watched her carefully to see if she was "putting on a front"—she was not. She somehow developed the uncanny ability to suppress her own grief to lift the burdens for other people.

Many people have mused over my mother's strength. When I asked her about it, she was very casual and thought everyone was making a big deal out of nothing. "What choices did I have? They were dead and there wasn't anything I could do to bring them back." I couldn't help but contrast my mother's demeanor to the woman who draped herself over the closed coffin and refused to allow the mortician to bury her deceased husband. The family of the former accepted death and went away rejoicing that we still had Mom and each other. The family of the latter stood back in shocked horror. They seemed to feel absolutely helpless in trying to bring some closure to the life of their father. I felt genuine sorrow for the widow and her entire family.

After the hubbub of the funeral is over and life begins to return to normal, what do you do? From observations, I would suggest that you not rush into anything. An increasing number of fraudulent characters prey on newly widowed women and men. They are more than willing to help you invest the proceeds from insurance policies, life's savings, or investments. They promise big returns that will ensure financial security for you and your family for the rest of time. A safeguard for you is to know that time is on your side. When your mind has had a chance to clear, you are in a better position to make wise business decisions.

If the person pressuring you to invest tells you it is a "once in a lifetime deal" and it sounds too good to be true, it is probably because it isn't true. Good deals come along all the time. Whenever anyone wants to hurry you to invest, you ought to contact your clergy, an attorney, your children, or a trusted family friend. Get their advice before doing anything.

After life has returned to normal, contact your accountant and have him draw up a summary sheet of where you are financially and what the projected monthly income will be. Chances are by this time in your life, your home will be paid for. You may find that your financial requirements are not as great as you first thought. It is very likely that you will have much more money coming in monthly than you need to meet your basic needs. Then investment is something you do only if *you* want to do it. It is not something you have to do in order to ensure stability.

You have already been cautioned many times not to give your credit card number to just anyone—especially over the phone. You need not respond to those who tell you that in order to claim a large prize that you have won without even entering the contest, you need to send a large sum of money to some post office box number. Scamming seniors out of their life's savings seems like a cheap, low trick for even the unscrupulous. But there are those around who do not care about you or your future—just your money.

Assuming you have insulated yourself from such characters, what do you do? Many widows or widowers decide to put a new face on their home. Carpets are changed, wallpaper replaced, cabinets refaced, woodwork painted or restained, light fixtures replaced, television sets replaced, and so on. Especially if the beloved spouse who recently passed away was ill, you may have postponed any improvements to make sure the lingering illness did not completely deplete your financial reserves.

My paternal grandmother and grandfather had a happy married life (not without challenges, but relatively happy). After Grandpa's passing, Grandma completely overhauled her home. It seems Grandfather had controlled the purse strings all of their married life, even to the purchasing of Grandma's dresses and clothes. Now she was free to make those choices she had been denied for so many years. She had really good taste and now had the freedom and funds to show them off. We all thought it was great—so did she.

If your health is good and you have the interest, traveling is a wonderful option. It will not be difficult to find others like you who have the means but not a companion to travel with. There are tours that cater to seniors. Many great and lasting friendships can be made on such excursions. After fifteen years, my mother was still corresponding with a couple of single women who live in Singapore. They met while on a trip to Norway and Sweden. Faithfully every Christmas and on their birthdays, she sent cards and letters. They remember her birthday and holidays as well. They never met again in this life, but that one brief time they spent together has enriched all of their lives.

Even if you are not up to international travel, you may find local and interstate tours exciting and not too physically demanding. Traveling to see children and grandchildren does not have to stop just because your spouse has passed away. The interest alone on your savings accounts may be sufficient to finance your travels. If the pace of the tour is too rigorous, make sure you look more carefully next time. You'll then know the questions to ask before signing up.

For many, being alone is a difficult adjustment. They are accustomed to having people around and do not like the solitude. There are retirement communities and homes available. Seniors eat together, go shopping together, go to movies together, recreate together, and yet enjoy the privacy of their own quarters.

Others enjoy the solitude. Too many people, too much noise, and too many activities make them nervous. There isn't a right or a wrong. It is a matter of personal preference. Your decision is not set in concrete. You may decide to stay at home for a few years and then move to a retirement home. It may be somewhat more difficult to go in the reverse. However, just because it is difficult does not mean you can't do it. If you have the resources and the desire to buy another home and move out of your condo or retirement home, you are free to do it. Then if you decide you liked it where you were, you can always sell it and move back to the retirement community. The choice is yours.

Change may bother you. Travel may not be of interest to you. You may opt for the familiar routine you have known for years. That is perfectly all right. Children may want to make your decisions for you. If you are still healthy in body and mind, it shouldn't be too difficult to call them together and re-establish yourself as the captain of your own ship. My mother was in her nineties and "didn't take guff from anybody!" When she put her foot down, we had pretty well concluded that she would do whatever she pleased.

There may come a time in your life when you are more interested in just staying home than in being out and about. Just a word of caution. Don't become such a recluse that if something happened to you, no one would come by to check on you because you have shut them out of your world. Even daily contact from your friends on the telephone will give you the peace of mind that someone will always be there in case of an emergency. There are apps to ensure you are checked in on daily or more often and will summon help if you don't respond.

Will you choose to marry again after you've lost a mate? That is entirely up to you. It may be somewhat difficult on your children and grandchildren if you marry and start a new, active life. However, many seniors are finding happiness and fulfillment in their next mate. Many of the issues that were so difficult when we were young are non-issues later in life. The prospects of having additional children is generally not a concern. The combining of two very different families is of greater concern. There may be twice as many children and grandchildren to remember at Christmas and birthdays. It is a little more complicated when inviting the family over for Thanksgiving or Christmas dinner. Complicated but not impossible. Some enterprising families hold two Thanksgiving dinners, one on the traditional Thursday and another on Friday. Since both days are generally holidays, it does not impact work schedules. Since there is still a two-day weekend after Friday, travel home is not generally an issue. If the families either don't get along, or there are too many when everyone gets together (more likely), or the families have nothing in common but you, it may be wiser to hold separate celebrations.

Some seniors have very successfully integrated both families into their new life together. Because some marriages later in life are not positive, it might be wise to keep your estates separate for inheritance purposes. That is a decision that only the two of you can make. Although it is rare, there have been seniors who prey on other seniors and marry just to get their hands on the estate. Although not common, that kind of betrayal is almost worse than a fraudulent shyster. When a person uses love as a deceptive tool, even the strongest feel betrayed. It is only a caution flag that you need to consider before combining assets.

What do you do if the children or grandchildren are adamantly opposed to your marrying again? Ultimately, after their objections have been analyzed, the decision is yours. If you decide to marry over their objections, talk with them and ask for their understanding and support. In the unlikely event that they will give neither, you must make the final decision. Some families who opposed remarriage have softened later when they noticed how happy she was. It is very selfish to expect you to live in loneliness because no one can replace Grandpa or Grandma. Their lack of maturity should not inhibit you from finding happiness and fulfillment.

If you decide to marry and things do not go well, you are mature enough to undo your mistake. Marriages are broken as well as made. It would be a mistake of the first magnitude to stay in a marriage that was bringing sorrow and unhappiness, after you have given it your all. You deserve to have as much happiness as possible during the final years of your life. Hopefully, the lessons you have learned over a lifetime will contribute to your contentment in marriage rather than a continuation of bitterness and disappointment.

Enough about marriage. What is there in life after the death of a spouse? The answer to that question suggests that you stand back and take another "fix" on your goals for life. Are there any areas of life where you haven't successfully completed what you wanted to accomplish? Perhaps there are areas where you hadn't really considered what you wanted to accomplish while you were so busy bearing and rearing children, making a living, being active in community and civic service, being involved in church service, and the like. As you stand back from the hustle and bustle of life, you will be constrained to admit that your days in mortality are getting fewer with the passage of time. It, therefore, becomes an imperative issue to decide how you want to spend your time.

In a way, the death of your spouse has simplified matters. You no longer have to consider his or her needs. It is just you and your dreams. Generally, a radical departure from your lifelong course is not a wise thing. However, if your spouse was less than perfect (which all of us are), it might be an appropriate time to change. If your circle of friends had been the "party" type and you realize that it would be very easy to resort to the bottle as an escape from the pains of living in reality, then a radical change might be for your benefit. If your former circle of friends does everything as couples, you will obviously be "odd man out." Square dancing without your partner is not the most fulfilling activity. You may either find another partner or change your activities. I think you catch the drift of what I am trying to say.

Life necessitates changes. You may not have liked some activities before the death of your spouse but are less resistant to them now as a widow. To your amazement, you may find that the new activity is even more satisfying than anything you have participated in up to this time. My urging is not to categorically turn down opportunities just because you've never done them before or because you don't think you'd be interested in them. A second urging, don't make a decision after the first time. Almost all new areas are uncomfortable or even frightening for the first few times we participate in them. If you will give the activity an honest try, your initial reaction may be the opposite of your present satisfaction. Let life "grow" on you. If the initial months after the honeymoon were an indication of what the rest of married life would be like, would you have stuck it through? Probably not. But bugs and wrinkles are worked out, and with a lot of work, married life may have been the greatest thing you engaged in. Life after the death of a spouse is no different.

I have a genuine concern for those who believe that their life, their happiness, their ability to accomplish anything they desire is inextricably tied to another person. You can literally accomplish anything you want. While it is true that it may have been more fun or easier to accomplish what you wanted to with your mate, it is not true that your mate's passing precludes you from undertaking whatever venture your mind can conceive.

Are you too old to do an activity? That's up to you! Are you too shy, too submissive, too anything to do whatever you want to do? Only if you tell yourself you are. I have seen seniors enjoying the view from the highest mountains I have ever climbed. I have ridden with single seniors on airplanes traveling around the world. I have sat by single seniors at ball games, concerts, operas, banquets, and lectures. I can't think of anything

I've done where there haven't been single seniors in attendance. If there is a ceiling placed on you concerning what you can accomplish, it must be self-imposed.

Just as you stepped through that uncertain door called marriage, so you can step through that uncertain door entitled "life after the death of a spouse." As there was life after the marriage ceremony, so there is life after the funeral ceremony. Decide to make life happen.

Chapter 16

ON THE OTHER SIDE OF DEATH'S DOOR

At least part of the fear of dying is the uncertainty of what lies on the other side of death's door. Is there really a next life? What will it be like? Many years ago, my aging grandmother, said, concerning her reluctance to die, "I know what life here is like. I'm not sure what life over there will be like!" Perhaps you may not believe in a life after death. Or you may have a sure knowledge that mortal life is not the end of existence. No matter where you are on the continuum from "no belief" to "sure knowledge," I presume you are not closed to entertaining some new ideas.

If one is inclined to believe what has been written in the Bible, it must be concluded that mortality is like a thin slice of meat between two very fat rolls. The Lord, in explaining His prophetic call to the prophet Jeremiah said: "Before I formed thee in the belly I knew thee; and before thou camest forth out of the womb I sanctified thee, and I ordained thee a prophet unto the nations" (Jeremiah 1:5). The Lord also explained to Moses: "Remember the days of old, consider the years of many generations: ask thy father, and he will shew thee; thy elders, and they will tell thee. When the most High divided to the nations their inheritance, when he separated the sons of Adam, he set the bounds of the people according to the number of the children of Israel" (Deuteronomy 32:7–8). Was birth the beginning? Not for Jeremiah, the children of Israel, or the sons of Adam (meaning the entire human race). Even during New Testament times, the Apostle Paul declared, as he confirmed and elaborated upon what God had revealed to Moses: "And [God] hath made of one blood all nations of men for to dwell on all the face of the earth, and hath determined the times before appointed, and the bounds of their habitation" (Acts 17:26).

It seems from the above scriptures and others that we lived with God before coming to this earth. Even to the beleaguered Job, the Lord asked a probing question suggesting a life before mortal birth: "Where wast thou when I laid the foundations of the earth? declare, if thou hast understanding. Who hath laid the measures thereof, if thou knowest? or who hath stretched the line upon it? Whereupon are the foundations thereof fastened? or who laid the corner stone thereof; When the morning stars sang together, and all the sons of God shouted for joy?" (Job 38:4–7). It may have been a rhetorical question, or more likely Job understood that he lived before. Who are the "sons of God" spoken of in this scripture? John, Christ's beloved apostle, taught the eternal truths his Master had taught him. He said: "Behold, what manner of love the Father hath bestowed upon us, that we should be called the sons of God: therefore the world knoweth us not, because it knew him not. Beloved, now are we the sons of God, and it doth not yet appear what we shall be: but we know that, when he shall appear, we shall be like him; for we shall see him as he is" (1 John 3:1–2).

As you have observed your children and other people, it seems evident that they came into life "pre-programmed." Even though your children may have had the same father and mother, they are uniquely different. From Paul's teaching to the Athenians, it seems apparent that God even determined when and where, and how far we would travel on earth before we were ever born. One may be tempted to ask, "Well, if my whole life was planned out before I was born, what is the use of living?" It is helpful if we understand the difference between predestination and foreknowledge. Predestination is forcing you to act or be a certain way, without any choice on your part. Foreknowledge is God's unique ability to know the end from the beginning (see Isaiah 46:10). Just because He knows something does not necessarily mean that He causes it to happen. You are still free to choose. Volumes have been written about the omniscience (all-knowing nature) of God. Suffice it to say for this writing, He does know all things but does not coerce any of His children (you and me) to act against our wills or in a predestined way.

Having introduced the idea of a pre-earth life, let us consider the purpose of life here on earth. Are we sent here by God just to exist until we die? Hardly. I cannot conceive that an all-knowing, all-powerful God would do anything by chance or without a purpose (see Ecclesiastes 3:1, 17). What is His purpose in having us sent here? Could it be to gain experiences that we could gain in no other way? As the Savior outlined to His concerned disciples when He was about to depart, "Let not your heart be troubled: ye believe in God, believe also in me. In my Father's house are many mansions: if it were not so, I would have told you. I go to prepare a place for you. And if I go and prepare a place for you, I will come again, and receive you unto myself; that where I am, there ye may be also" (John 14:1–3).

What a promise! As we have discussed throughout this book, life is a time to gain experiences. We may not have done very well on all the varied tests of life, but we have probably done the best we knew how with the amount of knowledge we possessed at the time. In a time yet future, we will all stand before God to be judged for what we did here on the earth. John the Revelator said, "And I saw the dead, small and great, stand before God; and the books were opened: and another book was opened, which is the book of life: and the dead were judged out of those things which were written in the books, **according to their works**. And the sea gave up the dead which were in it; and death and hell delivered up the dead which were in them: and they were **judged every man according to their works**" (Revelation 20:12–13, emphasis added).

If we seriously consider the implication of a future judgment, then it would seem practical to expend whatever energy is necessary to make preparations for that judgment. How? By living the best that our knowledge teaches us. As we continue our quest for an understanding of truth, more truth is opened to our minds. For example, if you had parenting to do all over again and knew at the beginning of your experience what you know now, how much better could you do? If there are changes you can see you would make, then you have grown and progressed since you were in that condition. Thankfully, we will be judged according to the light we had at the time we passed through each phase of life.

Since a judgment awaits us when we pass on to the next life, it seems self-evident that this life then becomes a time when we can and should make preparations to meet God. How do we prepare? Jesus responded to the rich young man who questioned Him about how to gain eternal life, by saying: "And he said unto him, Why callest thou me good? there is none good but one, that is, God: but if thou wilt enter into life, keep the commandments (Matthew 19:17, Mark 10:19). That injunction (to keep the commandments) is given so many times in the holy scriptures that it would take pages to record all of the references. Since you can't obey what you don't know, it seems like a good idea to keep searching the scriptures and learning all we can about God's plan for us and what His expectations of us are.

Some people argue that salvation comes to every person who professes Jesus as the Christ. Others contend that good works are required for salvation. Rather than enter into a lengthy scriptural argument (since both positions have scriptural support), would we be better situated to consider a combination of grace and works? Perhaps we must do all within our power (which never would be enough to merit salvation) and then plead for the grace of God to make up the difference. Are we saved by grace? Absolutely! How do we reconcile that position with James 2:24, which reads, "Ye see then how that by works a man is justified, and not by faith only"? It is simple if we combine the two concepts—we are saved by grace after all we can do.

If we assume that we are saved totally by grace without anything other than a declaration of our acceptance of Jesus as the Christ, and then discover that God requires certain works of us, we could be in dire straits. If we strive to fulfill the required works of the gospel and find that nothing but faith is required to trigger the grace of God, what have we lost? Even the Savior warned at the conclusion of the Sermon of the Mount: "Not every one that saith unto me, Lord, Lord, shall enter into the kingdom of heaven; but he that **doeth** the will of my Father which is in heaven" (Matthew 7:21, emphasis added).

Does death end the learning process? Is there progress after death? Can changes in our attitude and behavior be made after we die, or is everything set in concrete when we exit this life? Those are valid questions that require us to peek behind the door of death to see the condition of those who have gone on before, in order to ascertain the answers. We have already noted that in John 14:1–3 the Savior said there were many mansions in the house of His Father, which He promised to go and prepare for us. The writer of Ecclesiastes said, "Then shall the dust return to the earth as it was: and the **spirit shall return unto God who gave it**" (Ecclesiastes 12:7, emphasis added). Again, the scriptures suggest that we "return unto God." How can we return where we have never been? Another scriptural verification of a life with God before being born on this earth. However, the scripture also teaches what happens to man at the time of death.

The body and the spirit together make the person or the soul of man. A baby born without its spirit is called a "stillbirth." As long as the body and spirit are united, the person is living. When the spirit separates from the body, we call that death. The body decomposes into elements common to this earth. It returns to the dust of the earth, scripturally speaking. However, the spirit of man continues to live.

Before we were born on this earth we could rightly have been called an "unembodied spirit." During our earthly stay, we can rightly be called an "embodied spirit" or a spirit clothed with a mortal body. Following death, because we had once possessed a body, we could rightly be termed a "disembodied spirit." At some future time, our spirit will take up again our body and be known as a "resurrected spirit." Yes, we will have a physical body as a resurrected being, but it will be enlivened by our eternal spirit that has always existed.

When we begin to view ourselves as eternal beings, life takes on a whole new meaning. We didn't start at birth. We had developed a unique personality even before we were born. We continue to develop our personality, character, and intellect while here in mortality. Our loved ones (as well as ourselves) continue to exist in the next life with the same personality and character they possessed here. When we meet them again, we will know them as well or better than we knew them during their mortal lives. They may have improved greatly beyond what we remember.

Whatever we may have been taught before, the scriptures clearly teach that life continues beyond the grave. Although the body lies in the grave, the eternal part of man—the spirit—continues on as an individual, conscious entity. The Apostle Peter enlarged our understanding of the space between death and the resurrection.=: "For Christ also hath once suffered for sins, the just for the unjust, that he might bring us to God, being put to death in the flesh, but quickened by the Spirit: By which also he went and preached unto the spirits in prison" (1 Peter 3:18–19). The purpose for the Savior's teaching the spirits in prison is explained in the next chapter. Continuing, Peter said, "For for this cause was the gospel preached also to them that are dead, that they might be judged according to men in the flesh, but live according to God in the spirit" (1 Peter 4:6). If it were not possible for people to continue to learn and change in the next life, why would Christ have taught them His gospel? I am convinced by holy scriptures that God never stops trying to help us improve even after death. He does this by teaching us His holy laws and then allows us agency to choose to obey or disobey them. That includes the next life as well as this one.

Given the continued opportunity to learn after death, one of the great questions of the equity or fairness of God is resolved. How can God be a fair God and a just God and yet allow only a small portion of His children (considering the whole of mankind since the beginning) to ever have an opportunity to hear His laws? Since we are to be judged according to our works, it would seem unfair to judge people and condemn them for not living laws they have never known. The teaching of the gospel in the next life gives everyone an equal opportunity to be judged against the gospel standards. There is so much more to say about this topic, but perhaps that is sufficient for the purpose of this book.

One may be somewhat put off by Peter's use of the term "spirits in prison" since the only thing we have to compare the word "prison" to is a correctional institution. However, could it be termed a "prison" because there are places they cannot go and things they cannot do rather than a building with bars on the windows and locks on the doors? I am in prison as a mortal regarding playing the piano if I don't know how to play. After learning to play, I am freed from my non-physical prison. I am in a kind of prison regarding the world of computers if I don't know how to use them. When I learn to use that great resource, the prison doors swing open and I am free to travel to the limits of my understanding of computers. You can see that the term "prison" may have a much different connotation that we generally associate with it.

Having the gospel preached in the next life opens the prison doors and sets captive spirits free. But what is the key that opens those prison doors? The Bible holds the answers to what that something is. When Nicodemus asked the Savior what he had to do to gain eternal life, the scriptures record: "Jesus answered, Verily, verily, I say unto thee, Except a man be born of water and of the Spirit, he cannot enter into the kingdom of God" (John 3:5). It seems apparent that baptism constitutes the gate or door through which a person must pass before they can enter into the kingdom of God. But countless, nameless billions have died without having had an opportunity to be baptized. What of them? The Apostle Paul alluded to a practice common in the primitive Christian church, which most churches today do not practice. "Else what shall they do which are **baptized for the dead**, if the dead rise not at all? why are they then baptized for the dead?" (1 Corinthians 15:29, emphasis added). It was common practice in the early Christian church for living members of the church to be baptized by proxy for those who had died without baptism. Then, if they responded favorably in the next life to the gospel being taught to them, they could enter the kingdom of God. The inference being that if they did not choose to accept the gospel in the next life, the proxy baptism would do them no good at all. That would be the same as if a person in this life was baptized but did not conform his life to the teachings of the gospel. His baptism would not be valid, and he would subsequently be denied entrance into the kingdom of God. The performing of the ordinance of baptism, whether personally while alive on this earth, or performed by others after the person has died, according to the scriptures, opens the doorway to heaven and continued life with God.

You may recall that the Savior promised the thief on the cross, "Verily I say unto thee, To day shalt thou be with me in paradise" (Luke 23:43). Perhaps the word "paradise" would be more correctly translated "world of spirits." The Apostle Paul, recounting some of the spiritual visions he had enjoyed during his lifetime said, "How that he was caught up into paradise, and heard unspeakable words, which it is not lawful for a man to utter" (2 Corinthians 12:4). From all that has been written in scriptures, it seems that the next phase of life is not a place to be feared. It is a place of learning and growing. It is a place where we can continue the perfecting process in preparation for a still future resurrection and judgment. Remember what John the Revelator said, that the graves would have to yield up the bodies they have held captive and the spirit world (hell) would have to yield up the spirits of the dead (see Revelation 20). That is the description of the resurrection. Then judgment would take place. Although Revelation 20 describes those who will be filthy still at the time of the resurrection and thus described their temporary residence in the spirit world as "hell," it also tells of those who were faithful to Christ during their earthly life and thus had spent their time in the spirit world in a state of happiness or paradise. The wicked will be eventually cast into outer darkness and suffer the second death. The righteous will be able to live with Christ and God eternally (see Revelation 21).

Are we then to be reunited with our loved ones who have passed away? Most certainly! From what has been written in the New Testament, it seems like that time will not be too far distant. Paul instructed the saints at Thessalonica about a time we call the great Second Coming of Christ: "For the Lord himself shall descend from heaven with a shout, with the voice of the archangel, and with the trump of God: and the dead in Christ shall rise first: Then we which are alive and remain shall be caught up together with them in the clouds, to meet the Lord in the air: and so shall we ever be with the Lord" (1 Thessalonians 4:16–17).

The mind begins to reel as we contemplate the promises made to those who try to live the best they know how. Even if we die (or our loved ones die), we will be reunited at the Second Coming. Those who are still alive here on the earth will be "caught up." That is often referred to as "the Rapture." Those who are dead will receive their bodies again as resurrected beings. Those who are alive will be changed somewhat to enable their bodies to withstand the brightness of His glory (see 2 Thessalonians 2:8).

In trying to make clear and understandable the great plan of God concerning His children, I do not want to infer that God will look at the mistakes we make knowingly and ignore them. It would be to our eternal credit if we would take inventory of everything we are doing that may be offensive to God or contrary to His commandments and change our behavior to conform.

On the other hand, it would be an unfair portrayal of what the scriptures teach, to suggest that if we are not perfect, there is no hope for us in the next life. The one teaching that must ring clear and without question is that there is a life following this one. Whether we embrace that teaching or not does not make the teachings of the scriptures of none effect. One might as well deny the law of gravity and jump off a building expecting not to fall to the ground and receive some injury, as to believe that our denial of life after death would result in our being exempted from entering into that life in preparation for a future judgment.

What we believe is really of little consequence. What God has revealed is truth and will never change. What a comfort to know that we are not put here on earth to wander aimlessly without any knowledge of where we came from before birth. Equally comforting is the revealed knowledge of why we are here and how we are able to pass the test of life. Thrilling beyond description is the revelation of what lies ahead. All of those tender feelings that we developed for our loved ones here on earth will be renewed and amplified in the next life. Armed with that confidence, why should we view death as anything other than what it is, a graduation from mortality into a state of eternal life?

As you approach death yourself, or as a loved one approaches death, it would be well to remember the Savior's calming counsel to His disciples as He approached that uncertain door. We have referred to this scripture once, but it seems appropriate to end this chapter with the Savior's words: "Let not your heart be troubled: ye believe in God, believe also in me. In my Father's house are many mansions: if it were not so, I would have told you. I go to prepare a place for you. And if I go and prepare a place for you, I will come again, and receive you unto myself; that where I am, there ye may be also" (John 14:1–3).

Chapter 17

IS IT WORTH THE PRICE?

When a person stands at the conclusion of a huge, difficult project (or even a small one) and looks back at what has been accomplished, there is a justifiable sense of pride or satisfaction. Seldom is it the easy tasks that bring the greatest satisfaction. So it is with life. The longer the battle, the more difficult the obstacles, the more trying the circumstances, the more thrill comes as we mentally review our lives.

The youth use a phrase to indicate that a person has a problem with their outlook on life. They say, "That person has an attitude!" At first, I thought, "Everyone has an attitude. What is the big deal?" After listening to them and asking questions, it became apparent that "having an attitude" was not given as a compliment. In talking with health care personnel, caregivers, and from personal experience, it is apparent that "having an attitude" is not reserved strictly for the young. Some seniors seem to delight in making life as miserable for those who attend to them as they are themselves. What a shame. At the very time in life when they are poised to do the most good, they take the easy route that requires little or no discipline. Anyone can be a "destroyer." Gossiping, maliciously putting stumbling blocks in the path of those who follow, and acting in such a way that results in additional work for those attending to them are all tactics used by some seniors to derive whatever small pleasure comes from making others suffer. I wonder if they have never tasted how sweet it is to be a builder? When one's objective is to lift, improve, increase, help, promote, and mentor everyone they interact with, the resultant joy goes beyond description. Contrasting the pleasure of tearing down with the joy of building up should give adequate testimony of the comparative value of building.

The world does a pretty good job of tearing people down. It really does not require our help. So here we stand, as it were, near the finish line in the race of life. We only have one finish to make. Will we succumb to the temptation to make people as miserable as others may have made us? Or will we break the vicious cycle and try to make life easier and more enjoyable for those who follow? The choice is ours, but we can't have it both ways.

Your vision of life has been expanded by the experiences you have had. Wisdom cannot be taught in a classroom. A person can gain a lot of "knowledge" by going to school, being an apprentice, reading books, watching television, talking with others, or attending lectures. But how to use that knowledge to your own and others' advantage is what really constitutes wisdom. Some of the smartest people I know (they have a lot of knowledge), are the dumbest (they lack the wisdom to apply their knowledge).

One modern example will demonstrate the principle. Young people who have grown up with computers find little or no difficulty mastering the principles that have the potential to improve their own and everyone else's lives. We who may not be as "computer literate" stand back in amazement. An alarming number of these young people are becoming hackers. A hacker is a person who illegally breaks through the security codes on the computers in large corporations or governments and destroys or wrongfully uses the data stored there. They have successfully broken into banks and stolen large amounts of money. They have erased data from research laboratories, thus postponing medical discoveries that will eventually benefit millions of people. They have broken into top-secret governmental computers and stolen secrets that could jeopardize national security. All of this is a game to them. An innocent kid's game. When they are caught, however, they are tried and imprisoned as common criminals.

Of what value was their knowledge? If they had channeled their knowledge in the right direction, there is no telling what contributions they could have made. Instead, their knowledge was used to make life more difficult for others, to hurt, to rob, to destroy, and to get personal gain at the expense of everyone else. I wonder what these "whiz kids" are thinking as they sit in prison wasting their lives. Have they seen the error of their ways? Are they just going to be more bitter when they are released and engage in something even more destructive? Only time will tell.

I have watched people as they near the end of their involvement in a large project sit back and idle away their time. When asked why they were not productively working, the response reveals the shallowness of their commitment. "Why should I work so hard? I'm not going to be here to benefit directly from my labors." They rationalized that because no one had sacrificed for them before they arrived, they were not going to expend the energy for those who were following. I was hard pressed to figure out the logic. They had a certain amount of time to put in on the project. Personal integrity would suggest that they "give a day's work for a day's pay." They seemed to sense no higher cause than their own selfish gratification and self-interest.

You may recognize that my example is the definition of life. Life (the great project) was in progress when we arrived, and it will continue after we are gone. Although others may not have "smoothed the way" very well for you, if you have read any history at all, you will have to admit that the worst conditions into which you may have been born were far superior to those of a few hundred years ago. It is not a correct analysis to say that no one did anything for you. Your indoor plumbing, electricity, telephones, cell phones, computers, televisions, cars, airplanes, packaged food, modern medicine, and the list goes on *ad infinitum*, were all given to you without your personal input. To say in return that you have no obligation to those who follow is surely a manifestation of our failure to see life in proper perspective.

If we say, "Well, we will not directly benefit from our efforts to better mankind, because we will be dead," we also reveal our lack of eternal vision. What if life does not end at death? What if the rewards for your works (both good and bad) follow you? Then life is not the totality of existence. Just as high school grades determined whether a young person could go to college and where they could gain admittance, what if our actions determine where we spend our time in the next life? No, life is too short and too valuable to become egocentric (totally self-centered). At this prime time when the torch to lead others is in your hand, you owe it to yourself to hold it up (even when it hurts) and lead the way. Let the future bring what it may, so instead of trying to "kill time," why not try working it to death?

What if you have erred in the direction you have taken to this point in your life? Is all lost? Can an old dog learn new tricks? Only an old dog can determine that. There isn't anything stopping him. It is never too late to turn one's face toward God. Even on the final day of life, it would be better to be headed in the right direction than to exit life facing in the wrong direction. The blessing of life is that each day starts with a *tabula rasa*—a blank slate. We do not have to write on the slate what was written yesterday. It is patently impossible to write tomorrow's entry today. Today is all we have. What is to prevent me from being closer to the person I want to be today than I was yesterday? Habits are hard to break—hard, but not impossible. Obstacles are difficult to overcome—difficult, but not insurmountable. Relationships require effort to strengthen—effort, but achievable. So it is with every issue in life you care to tackle. Is it worth it? Only eternity can answer that question completely.

I remember wondering on many occasions whether all the class work, all the papers, all the nights of missed sleep, all the worry, all the tests, and all the time I spent away from my family was worth it to get a doctorate degree. Many times I was "absolutely sure" the sacrifices were not worth it. But I couldn't quit. What would people say? Probably for the entirely wrong reason, I kept going. The day my colleagues and I walked across the platform to be "hooded" and awarded our degrees, the question I had asked many times before had a change of answers. It was all worth it! During the ordeal, I would have argued against myself. At the graduation ceremony, I was willing to admit that I had been hasty in making my evaluation. Could life be like working on your "doctorate of life" degree? Someday I will try to find the one person who dropped out of our doctoral program. I want to ask him if he ever regretted not trudging along to the end of the project that he originally committed to. There were over three hundred applicants for sixteen positions in the doctoral program. He took one of them at the exclusion of the other two hundred and eighty-four people. Then he dropped out. He is a good guy. I am not passing judgment on him. But his unwillingness to complete the course had deprived himself of the degree, his family of the additional opportunities that come from having the degree, the institution who denied the others the opportunity to participate, the colleagues he had worked with and been committed to, and the world who could have benefited from his research. It seems we were all losers when he didn't follow through and endure to the end.

Will we see the same scenario if we fail to follow through faithfully in life? How far reaching will the negative effects of our failure go? If you consider what difference it may have made to you if your grandparents had been everything you had hoped they would be, can you sense that your grandchildren may say the same thing about you? Legacies, traditions, family characteristics, and reputations all depend on what you do during the final years of your life. The greatest gift you can give to your descendants is not gold and silver (they will soon be spent and may be foolishly wasted), but the gift of yourself. As you inconvenience yourself to teach your children and grandchildren, you are perpetuating your influence into the endless future. If you take the light that is intended to lead others and shine it in your own eyes, you will not only stumble yourself, but will fail to provide the guiding light for those who follow.

I remember running a race when I was beginning high school. I had not trained for the mile race, but the coach didn't have anyone else to run so I was assigned. I told him I didn't know how to run the race. He said, "Just stay in front of the guy behind you!" That seemed easy enough. The first two of the four laps around the track were fairly easy. None of the freshman runners were in good shape ,so it wasn't too difficult to stay in front of the guy right behind me. The third lap was more challenging. My lungs were burning and my leg muscles hurt. I thought I would just drop out of the race. Then I saw the coach's face. He was excitedly yelling at me to keep up the pace. I didn't want to disappoint him, so I kept on running.

At the beginning of the fourth and final lap, I knew I was in trouble. My leg muscles were starting to cramp, I felt numbness in my hands and arms, and my lungs were on fire. There was no way I could finish the race. However, I was just in front of the guy right behind me. The pace must not have been much more than a fast walk. I was finished. I couldn't go on. Even the anticipated "chewing out" by the coach was not sufficient to keep me involved in the self-destructive idiocy of this race. I was going to quit!

Then I saw them. The other team members, the cheerleaders, and the parents who had driven us to the meet. They were all lining the sides of the track, cheering and urging me on. Didn't they know how tired I was? Didn't they care that I was doing permanent damage to my muscles and would probably never walk again? Didn't they realize that the will to win had evaporated? Didn't they know it was virtually impossible to stay ahead of the guy right behind me any longer? I guess they didn't because they kept cheering and urging me on.

Well, I may as well die in the cause, I thought. Reaching down deep inside for strength I was sure was not there, and will power that I thought I had exhausted, I made a final burst for the finish line. I crossed the finish line and fell totally exhausted into the open arms of the coach. I had won the race! It was painful even to stand with the second and third place finishers to receive the award. It did take a few days before I could walk again without excruciating pain in my legs, but there was no permanent damage. My lungs didn't burn up. Feeling returned to my hands and arms. But I never ran another mile race.

Life is like a mile race. We are on the last lap. We are only racing against ourselves. When the muscles get so tired and sore that we're sure we cannot continue, we need to look around at those who are cheering us on. Some of them don't even know they are part of our cheering section. Some of them don't even want you to finish strong. But your vision must be more clearly focused than theirs. Grandchildren and other younger people need an example of one who refuses to give in. When they see your gnarled hands and wobbly knees, your worn-out running shoes, and your faltering steps, how can they justifiably say that the race is too hard and they're going to quit? After all, they see themselves as far superior to you. They cannot allow you to "show them up."

Doctors, caregivers, children, grandchildren, friends, and clergy may even tell you the race is too difficult. For me that is the final challenge to win the race. A certain satisfaction comes when you have done the impossible. If your cheering team is encouraging you to finish the race, let them help you along. So, with or without your cheering section, you can win the race and walk without pain to the winner's circle to receive your reward. From every indication of people who have had a peek into the next life and those experiences that have been written in the Bible, the prize is more than worth the pain. The Apostle Paul wrote: "But as it is written, Eye hath not seen, nor ear heard, neither have entered into the heart of man, the things which God hath prepared for them that love him (1 Corinthians 2:9).

There will be an increasing number of cheerleaders on the sidelines who will encourage you to quit the race. Even some misdirected medical doctors under the guise of reducing pain and suffering will offer to assist you off the track. Their total lack of eternal vision and their misdirected efforts to "help" you must be overridden by your vision of the finish line and the glory that awaits those who victoriously finish the race of life. Since the Perfect Example, Christ, was perfected by the things that He suffered, what makes us believe that we will be any different? Whenever I hear people say that life is tough, I am tempted to ask, "When compared to what?" What are our options? If the purpose of life is just to exist, then they are probably correct—life is tough. If the purpose of life is to polish us, then the rubbing, and scraping are necessary elements.

We must finish this race on faith. Without direct revelation, there is no way to know until you pass through the door of death whether what has been written in the Bible about the purpose of life and the glory that awaits you is really true. If it is true, you have everything to gain by finishing the race of life successfully. If it is not true and there is nothing beyond the grave (which I know is false), you will still have left a sterling example for those who are following. It is against my basic faith to even suggest that there is no life after death. The Spirit whispers over and over that Jesus is who He says He is. God is there. His plan for us (His children) is perfect and will not fail. The road may be long and painful, but in the end we will all be constrained to admit that He who constructed the road and allowed the obstacles to clutter our path really did know what He was doing.

Many years ago, I visited a friend whose parents were teaching at a high school in American Samoa. On the island there is a mountain called the Mapusaga Rainmaker. It is about fifteen hundred feet high and the sides almost vertical. There was then (and probably still is now) only one road that runs the length of the island. I considered that it must have been designed by the devil in hell and constructed by his helpers here on earth. It was one series of potholes after another. The road was not straight. It would jig and jog in seemingly senseless turns. Every time we would ride the bus to Pago Pago, we would complain about the grueling ride, the bruised kidneys, and the punishing bumps we had to endure.

During the Christmas break from school, my friend and I climbed the Rainmaker. From the top of the mountain I received one of the significant revelations of my life. The road that seemed too rough while riding the buses to town appeared perfectly smooth from our vantage point. The "senseless" turns took on new significance. The bush was so thick we couldn't see a dozen yards off the road. The road would turn to miss a rock that we couldn't see from ground level but was evident from our elevation. The road would make another turn to miss a bog hole, a village, a cliff, or any of a dozen other obstacles. What seemed so senseless from ground level made perfect sense from atop the mountain.

So it will be with life. All of the jigs and jogs of life that seem to have no purpose now will make perfect sense when we stand on top of the Rainmaker of life. From that point on, I never complained about the inconvenience of the road as I had done so many times before.

So, where do you go from here? You can lay this book aside and be the same person you were before. That may be good or not so good, but if your reading hasn't acted as a catalyst to generate some ideas for self-improvement and improvement of your world, then I have failed in my objective. If you have a ways to go because you haven't been as diligent at perfecting yourselves and your family as you might have been, don't despair. There is always time, whether in this life or in the life to come, to patch the holes in your ship and move ahead. It may not be where we are on the pathway to perfection that makes the difference. It may be the direction we are heading. Only you can determine whether a change is desirable.

You may disagree with some of the principles I have taught in the book. They may not fit your situation or your value system. You may discard them like any other philosophy you consider to be in error. However, before discarding them, consider your alternative and make sure it is taking you closer to your goals in life. My objective is not to convert you to my philosophy, but to help you enjoy life to the fullest and make every preparation you can for the next life. If you are having all of the impact on the lives of others you can possibly have, this world will rapidly become a better place to live, a safer and more promising world for your children and grandchildren.

If you will take the challenge to live until you die, you will find life more satisfying; you will see the beneficial results of enduring the crosses of life; you will become the anchor in the lives of those who follow; and you will enjoy the peace that surpasses all understanding. A challenge, a mission, a test, and an opportunity. That is what life is all about. Live it until you die.

Epilogue

I found this little piece a number of years ago that seems like a fitting ending to this book. John Longden is the author:

> Today is here. I will start with a smile, and resolve to be agreeable. I will not criticize. I refuse to waste my valuable time.
>
> Today has one thing in which I know I am equal with others—Time. All of us draw the same salary in seconds, minutes, hours—24 Golden Hours each day.
>
> Today I will not waste my time, because the minutes I wasted yesterday are as lost as a vanished thought.
>
> Today I refuse to spend time worrying about what might happen. I am going to spend my time making things happen.
>
> Today I am determined to study to improve myself, for tomorrow I may be wanted, and I must not be found lacking.
>
> Today I am determined to do things I should do. I firmly resolve to stop doing the things I should not do.
>
> Today I begin by doing and not wasting my time. In one week I will be miles beyond the person I am today.
>
> Today I will not imagine what I would do if things were different. They are not different. I will make a success with what material I have.
>
> Today I will stop saying, "If I had time," for I never will "find time" for anything—if I want time I must take it.
>
> Today I will act toward other people as though this might be my last day on earth. I will not wait for tomorrow. Tomorrow never comes.[1]

---

1. Conference Report, Apr. 1966, 39.

One final after-thought that summarizes the entire content of this book:

THE BRIDGE BUILDER

An old man, going a lone highway,
Came at the evening cold and gray,
To a chasm, vast and deep and wide,
Through which was flowing a sullen tide.
The old man crossed in the twilight dim-
That sullen stream had no fears for him;
But he turned, when he reached the other side,
And built a bridge to span the tide.

"Old man," said a fellow pilgrim near,
"You are wasting strength in building here.
Your journey will end with the ending day;
You never again must pass this way.
You have crossed the chasm, deep and wide,
Why build you the bridge at the eventide?"

The builder lifted his old gray head.
"Good friend, in the path I have come," he said,
"There followeth after me today
A youth whose feet must pass this way.
This chasm that has been naught to me
To that fair-haired youth may a pitfall be.
He, too, must cross in the twilight dim;
Good friend, I am building the bridge for *him*."[2]

—*Will Allen Dromgoole*

2. From Father: An Anthology of Verse (EP Dutton & Company, 1931).

About the Author

Randy Bott is married to the love of his life, Vickie (fifty years and counting). They have six children, sixteen grandchildren, and one great-granddaughter.

Brother Bott has degrees from Utah State University (a bachelor's in psychology and a master's in secondary education) and a doctorate degree in educational leadership from Brigham Young University. He has served as a bishop, in two stake presidencies, and as a mission president. He served his first mission in Samoa.

After he retired from BYU in 2012, he and his wife served missions at BYU–Hawaii and in Sydney, Australia. They are currently preparing for another mission.

Brother Bott taught in the Church Education System in Utah and North Carolina for twenty years, and nineteen years at BYU–Provo. He has authored many books and articles. His passion is teaching and counseling. He loves people and loves problem-solving and creating new programs to help people succeed.